This book is a love letter to anyone and everyone who's ever felt the slow burning sting of being alone and wondered what the hell to do about it.

Leading with heart and vulnerability, Leisse Wilcox clarifies the remarkable and transformative power that comes from embracing our aloneness and holding it close. *Alone* is a trojan horse of a book, infusing personal stories and anecdotes to demonstrate that feeling lonely may be a key that unlocks sovereignty, and that from the right perspective, our darker places are filled with light.

- Dr. Jeremy Goldberg, Author, Speaker, Behavioral Scientist

A magical elixir that not just every single person needs but probably EVERY PERSON. As a single person, this wildly amped up my self-reverence, wrapped me in self-appreciation, AND gave me greater compassion for all humans, especially for those in relationships that suck or who are in fear cycles about anything really. I can't help but sense the obvious empowerment, for those "trapped" humans in particular (which is probably most of us), as Leisse's words help us set down that fear and take back our lives with a loving surrender to our own soul's plans.

- Katherine Gramman, Soul Mentor + Conscious Business Owner

This book does not disappoint!! Leisse is a talented writer, allowing the reader to get lost in her relatable and highly entertaining experiences weaved alongside relevant strands of research. She has found a way to write about a topic that many individuals shy away from examining. This book not only allowed me to reflect on what being single really means to me, but it also gave me the tools to look at being alone in an entirely new light. I recommend this book to anyone, not just single people.

Dr. Jennifer Reynolds, PhD Public Health

Alone is that rare book that is both timely and timeless. Whether in the midst of a global pandemic or just being a human, the fear of being alone is real, and it's terrifying. But it doesn't have to be, and in this beautifully written book, Leisse masterfully delivers the tools to show you how.

- Craig Stanland, Reinvention Architect, TEDx Speaker and Best-Selling Author of
Blank Canvas: How I Reinvented My Life After Prison

Leisse's words are the cozy comfort of a warm blanket on a crisp day, countered with the tough love of a dear friend who finds humor and honesty through the roller coaster of life. She gives us, as women, permission to be fully human—to feel, to grieve, to laugh, to pause, to trust, to fear, to breathe, and ultimately, to grow. This book is a beautiful reminder to nourish the greatest love affair of all—the relationship with yourself.

- Allison Villa, Psychotherapist + Relationship Expert

The irony of *Alone* is the moment that you start reading Leisse's words, you see how masterfully she has begun to do the work on herself (and continues to do so). In turn, this "work" allows us to walk closely with her and begin to forge our own path for self-love. Before you know it, you are feeling less "alone" because it's obvious somewhere out there in the world there is somebody who COMPLETELY gets you. Leisse gets us. And, as always, it feels beautiful to be seen.

- Tyler Merritt, Author/Actor/Activist and Creator of The Tyler Merritt Project

Part memoir, part self-help guide, part love letter to anyone aching with loneliness, *Alone: The Truth + Beauty of Belonging* assures us that though we may not choose to be alone, we absolutely choose the meaning we ascribe to our solitude. Through potent reframes, e.g., *What if self-care became soul care? and It's the feeling you want, not the thing you want,* Leisse emboldens us to embrace the truth that "when you belong to yourself, you are never really alone."

- Dr. Karin Anderson Abrell, Psychologist, Author, Podcast Host

The quest to belong drives much of our behavior. Leisse is brilliant in sharing hard truths that are blunt (yet full of compassion) about this basic human need of belonging. I didn't realize how much I needed this book! Stray puzzle pieces of my life slipped into place with each chapter, and I felt warmly nudged to be more conscious of my life choices.

- Carolyn Swora, Workplace Culture Architect and Leadership Coach

Published in Canada, for Global Distribution by YGTMedia Co.

www.ygtmedia.co/publishing

To order additional copies of this book: publishing@ygtmedia.co

Edited by Christine Stock
Book design by Doris Chung
Cover design by Michelle Fairbanks
Cover Photography by Sara Tanner
ePub & Kindle editions by Ellie Silpa

TORONTO

ALONE

THE TRUTH + BEAUTY OF BELONGING

leisse wilcox

You only are free when you realize you belong no place—you belong every place—no place at all. The price is high. The reward is great.

-Maya Angelou

TABLE OF CONTENTS

INTRO

INTENTION OF THIS BOOK

There was just something about Valentine's Day 2020 that told me I did not want to, and really could not be, alone.

It was fresh after a few significant and back-to-back life events, including having finished chemo, undergoing body-altering and cancer-related surgery, and enduring the ongoing tremors of a traumatic divorce. My kids and I had been on the emotional roller coaster called "having our house for sale" for almost a year. It was during a planned relocation for our family . . . that, for reasons I don't wish to print in black and white, did not happen.

It was also three weeks before the world as we knew it would unimaginably and indelibly change overnight with the arrival of COVID-19, and in hindsight, I think there was a deep, intuitive *knowing* that culminated in low-grade anxiety around "another Valentine's Day *alone*."

I'd been single for a few years, yet being single on Valentine's had never bothered me before.

There was something about the massive number of life's changes/stops/ starts, though, that caused a pretty stark contrast between my expectations and my reality; it felt so dark and out of alignment with where I thought I would be by this point in my life, and as a conscious relationship coach who believes in her bones that the most significant relationship we have is the one we have with ourself, I knew I had to make a plan to care for myself from the inside out.

So, I made a plan.

I talked to some single gals who live in the city (close to family and that feels like home) that I had been thiiiiis close to relocating to. I invited them to join me in my home for dinner, and I would make us pizza and Pellegrino (my specialty), and we would listen to records and enjoy this (*stupid fucking Hallmark*) holiday together . . . and make it fun by making it our own.

They told me they'd love to BUT . . . they had already made plans to go to a drag show at a local brewery and that I should come along.

It was a yes for me.

Frankly, N O T H I N G sounded better to me than watching cute boys dressed in drag, while not so secretly watching cute boys dressed in plaid. I'd laugh, listen to Lady Gaga, and very likely give out my number to one (or two?) lucky and charming burly bearded guys.

I asked if the gals wanted me to grab the tickets, and they assured me that they had it all handled, so not to worry. Being intentional about letting go of my old (and icky) pattern of feeling like I needed to be in control, I took a deep breath and said great, thus allowing myself to be cared for, even in this tiny way, that had for so long been tough for me to wrap my head around.

A couple weeks later, I sent a casual hype text to my friend, saying how excited I was for our Galentine's Day plan, and where should I meet them? She wrote back with the news that the person who'd *sworn* she'd get the tickets didn't in fact get them, and now the show was sold out.

I was devastated.

At first blush, this situation may not sound like a big deal to you, but I had so much riding on that evening:
I had identified my own anxiety about being alone.
I took action to reframe it and put a (super fun) safety net plan in place.
I trusted someone else to help me execute this plan.

And then it didn't work out.

I called the brewery, effectively begging them to make an exception / put us on a cancellation list / sneak me in the back door. And when the answer was a resounding no / ha ha ha / definitely not, I had a mini panic attack. Then, I got my breathing back to a safe and tempered pace, put on my own coaching hat, and talked to myself the way I would talk to a client.

"Okay, sweet pea, I can see that you are very upset. Those feelings are real. I get it, and I am here for you. What is the story you're telling yourself right now? Is that story true? What do you need to feel supported?"

When I got quiet enough to listen, I found out the following:

What was the story I was telling myself?
Well, that I had been abandoned—again; that I would have to spend the evening alone, and that spending the evening alone would be a massive trigger to "still" being single almost five years post-divorce . . .

. . . *and that* that *was a failure.*

Bingo! There it was: The story I was telling myself that was *the* root of all this pain was that "single" was a *beacon of failure* in my personal life.

Was that story true?
Not reeaallly; people make mistakes, and not getting the tickets was one of them—more a metric of flakiness than of being abandoned. However, the trigger of "being alone = personal failure" felt *very* real and that was *very* worthy of my attention.

And what did I need to feel supported?
An amazing fucking evening that felt like a beautifully art-directed date night at home.

One of my greatest mindset hacks is to get clear on the feeling I want to cultivate, imagine and pretend what it is that leads to that feeling, then harness the feeling it gives me and implement what it is I was imagining and pretending. After all, we almost never want "the thing"; we want *the feeling* we think "the thing" is going to give us.

So, I imagined what a "perfect" date would look and feel like: wood-fired pizza, low candlelight, great music followed by something kinda silly and easy to watch on Netflix . . . and then "chill."[1] The feeling I imagined was low key, sexy, and fun in a beautiful, safe space that fostered genuine—not performative—intimacy. Then I *pretended* this "perfect" date was happening (with someone *other* than myself).

What would I need to create this scenario? I planned an outfit, I sourced zero-alcohol sparkling rosé, bought wood-fired pizza from this guy who makes them locally (frozen and ready for you to cook at home), made a playlist for dancing around the kitchen while said pizza was in the oven, and preplanned what to watch on Netflix that I knew would lead to "and chill"—and then I put it all into action.

I set the intention with myself to go on this amazing (solo) date and allow for compassionate space-holding (read: being cool to cry it the hell out) if at any point I felt triggered on the date.

....

1 That's a euphemism for "have sex." Just so we're clear here.

I dimmed the lights, lit the candles, burned the Palo Santo, and slipped into my fave ripped jeans, lace bralette with matching undies, and lowcut black cami. I did a neutral smoky eye and killer brows, spritzed on some Chanel, styled my hair, poured myself a drink in my long-stemmed champagne glass, and danced myself around the kitchen, listening to Motown.

I prepared my living room with more candles, lowered the lights, and set *Love Is Blind* to binge mode. I settled into my luxe leather sectional with pizza and my drink . . .

. . . and felt *really good.*

And in doing so? Feeling "really good" turned into a deep realization and appreciation that I had literally just created an entire evening that felt 100 percent like low-key, sexy fun in a beautiful safe space that fostered genuine, not performative, intimacy that you had better believe took me to my bedroom for a very "happy ending" to a very perfect evening. Meow.

And it kinda blew my mind.

I distinctly remember sitting on my couch and having the sudden awareness of knowing, without question, that being single actually felt really wonderful and pleasurable. So, maybe it wasn't "single" I was afraid of but rather the *alone-ness* of being single.

And that moment remains burned into my mind and emotional body:

If I wasn't afraid of being single, why the hell did being alone scare me so much?

We have this fairytale notion that maybe, if we meet the right person and have the right friends and don't fuck up our children too much, we won't die alone.

The zinger?
We are born alone, and we die alone.

Period.

I don't say these words to scare you but to gently guide you into the radical acceptance that this life, while we may share it with others at different times in different phases and in different chapters, this life is one of independent travel along our own unique and individual path.

When did "alone" become a four-letter word? What if we could start normalizing the human experience of being alone in a loving and focused way, therein offering so much comfort that this feeling of loneliness is not only a part of the human condition but is also a shared experience in feeling alone?

I have a recurring visual image that we are each walking along a path—all seven billion of us, walking seven billion individual paths. When you meet someone (for better or for worse), it feels like you're walking along the same path, but really, it's just that your individual paths are superimposed on top of one another.

This is true of our partners.
This is true of our kids.
This is true of our colleagues and clients.
This is true of our parents and friends.

There are moments (or long moments that feel like years, or really long moments that feel like decades) during which it seems that you are walking the same path as someone else until you get to that (mostly) inevitable fork in the road where you realize your paths are going in different directions.

Why? *Because you've been on your own path with its own direction this whole time, even when it felt shared.*

And your job in this life, at least one of your jobs, is to follow that path that *you alone* are capable of walking while living out the purpose, lessons, experiences, obstacles, and pleasure along the way.
That's it.
That's fact.
We are destined to walk alone, which isn't a bad thing.

So, what exactly are we afraid of? And why the hell are we afraid of it?

For me (and maybe even for you), being single has been a *part* of it, or should I say has played a part of it? And the part played by being single was more like a Trojan horse that was a brute force of an invitation to explore this concept of "alone" in this book. Because I bet you know as well as I do from your own life experience that the fear of being alone motivates a lot of people to make a lot of hella bad decisions in work, life, and love, like:

- staying in the wrong relationship for a really long time
- putting up with unkind / abusive / otherwise toxic family members
- hanging around deadbeat friends with borderline abusive or codependent personalities
- accepting less money than what you're worth
- generally setting (or following through on) few-to-no healthy, loving boundaries

These are all rooted in protecting ourselves from the fear of being alone.

In confronting my own deep-rooted fear of being alone, I learned a hard but life-changing lesson: *we are always alone.* And at the same time, we are never alone because we are always with ourselves. From first breath to last, and in every breath in between, the only person *guaranteed* to be there with you is YOU.

So, if we are never truly alone, then the feeling our "alone-ness" is masking, i.e., the deep desire to being and knowing that we are loved, completely reframes our sense of belonging because we always belong to ourselves, which is a profound sense of love and acceptance.

It's in our alone-ness and in our solitude where we discover just how whole we are, *which is the truth and beauty of belonging.*

And that is the intention of this book: to completely reexamine everything we know and feel about being alone in each major aspect of our lives, to reframe our alone-ness to the wandering feeling that we belong to ourselves, and to not only find the truth and beauty therein but to also revel in it and appreciate that while it is a solitary experience, it is also very much a shared emotional and human experience, which takes some of the pressure and weight off of feeling it all in isolation.

Being able to embody the sovereignty of what it means to be alone and reclaiming it as your own is paramount to strengthening the relationship you have with yourself. And the relationship you have with yourself is the platform upon which literally every other relationship is built, from work and money to life and love.

Because when you belong to yourself, and especially when you can see your Self as a part of something much, much bigger than yourself, the truth and beauty of it is that you are never really alone.

CONTEXT

I am forty years old, and my life doesn't look anything like I thought it would. I have

- three kids
- two cats
- one armpit-to-armpit scar across my chest where my breasts used to be
- zero husbands

I live in a town of fewer than 20,000 people and now, more than a year into the COVID-19 pandemic, I have no idea how the hell I'm going to meet someone who aligns with my values and vision.

The last time I had sex was two-and-a-half years ago, and it's safe to say that "it's starting to weigh on me."

I have been single for 2,007.5 days.

Technically, I have been in two relationships during that time, each lasting approximately forty-two days, each saying I love you too hard and too fast, each planning out the rest of our lives together—how we'd combine long-distance living or blending kids together and what "forever" would look like—within the first three weeks. Both of these relationships, plus a few almost / wished-they-were relationships along the way, were rooted in old and unhealthy patterns of codependency, and each were very much not the right fit with the right person.

I just found out that a consummate party guy I hooked up with one wild night is head over heels in love with and engaged to someone he met in an actual meet-cute on a film set.

I have ~~stalked scoped out checked in on casually glanced at~~ stalked the Instagram profile of someone I thought for sure was going to be *the guy* after an. entire. night. of. *ridiculously* hot sex followed by me making eggs in the morning, comfortable enough to just be myself in track pants and a messy bun, while he tenderly asked if we should check in on my elderly neighbor, only to be full on ghosted by him a couple weeks later.

I have checked my phone, casually, thirty-eight times in the last twenty-four hours just in case there's a text from a dude I have been not so secretly in love with for three years and to whom I communicated this love and who was not so secretly *non*reciprocal in his feelings for me. Turns out that there was a text: He met someone recently, and they're having a baby.

I have gone back and forth on writing this book 125 times, wondering if I'm the one—the very, very single one—to write a book about relationships, or the pain of being alone, while I am, in fact, alone.

A bunch of my old familiar fears started to rear their old familiar heads and told me I'm definitely not. That single or lonely women don't want to read a book by a single or lonely woman. Duh. They want to read about being single from a woman who is now truly, madly, deeply in love, with the engagement photo shoot on the beach to prove it, and who can fondly look back on her time being single with some assurance that, just like Snow White, someday her prince will come.

But then this other more healed, more loving, more confident part of me kicks in. The part that is a conscious relationship and master NLP coach, best-selling author, top podcast host, solo parent of three under ten, cancer survivor, accidental entrepreneur, relentless optimist, and taco enthusiast. That part kicks in and reminds me, not so subtly, that being alone is about *much more* than being single.

Plus, fucking *no one* wants to hear that someday a prince will come. You know why?

Because we don't know if that's true.

And that prospect? The possibility that "oh fucking shit, I might actually be single for now, for a while, forever, so mayyyyybe I should address the fears that come from there head on and start to look at where they come from and figure out how I'm going to make myself okay *EVEN*

IF I don't get the John Krasinski of my dreams that I've been waiting for," well, that needs to be considered.

In my first book, *To Call Myself Beloved*, I wrote a lot about facing fear by identifying it, labeling it, tracing it back to its roots, learning from it, healing it, thanking it for its presence, and moving the fuck on. It's a 386-page self-love manifesto, and I've used it to change the global conversation on emotional health and self-love across three continents, seventeen countries, and coast-to-coast provinces and states across Canada and the United States.

A large part of that manifesto was informed by me confronting what was, and still is, my deepest core wound and my darkest shadow:

The fear that I will never be loved by someone I feel is worthy of loving me.

Like in your face, fuck off, I will do anything and everything it takes to be with you because I see you and *value you* at your core love. And also, you're-kinda-pretty-and-make-me-laugh-my-fucking-face-off-and-we-like-all-the-same-things-and-more-importantly-*hate*-all-the-same-things-and-I-want-you-to-meet-my-family-and-go-to-the-cottage-with-yours-and-I-*really*-want-to-raise-your-kids-with-you-and-practice-making-a-whole-lot-more-and-then-get-up-and-make-you-tacos kinda love.

That extraordinary, simple, quiet, and real-deal everyday love.

This shadow remains a part of me, with all the things that happened in my past, and I lovingly refer to it as "my heart condition." This shadow feels like an emotional heart condition that needs me to be mindfully respectful of what kind of relationship I can or cannot thrive in and how to communicate my very specific boundaries, needs, and desires in a way that honors the conditions of my heart.

That's all good. The not-so-good thing is that somewhere along the line, in the wounding and subsequent healing, "alone" got equated with "unlovable," which is not the same thing at all, but because of my own deep wounding, it has often *felt* the same.

After years and years of healing, several tens of thousands of dollars in self-investment, and working with women and men across the globe in my conscious relationship mentorship and therapeutic coaching practice, you might think what I'm about to say is bad for business:

That wound is still there.

And just like I tell my clients, I am telling you here that when there is a deep fucking wound, like the kind that comes from your mother leaving your family when you were a baby and then again when you were a toddler and then a stepmom arrives who mentally and emotionally abuses you to the point of having Stockholm Syndrome while your dad buries himself in work and pretends not to see and then your ex's behavior during what was supposed to be a super peaceful divorce in which you lose almost every aspect of life as you knew it triggers C-PTSD until you get cancer and lose all your hair and then both breasts while solo parenting and running a business . . .

. . . you had better fucking believe that scar tissue gets left behind.

I have my own fair share of scar tissue, and I bet you do too.

Imagine that you cut your arm, and a little while later it heals. Sure, it was tender, but once the skin has healed over the wound, after having taken diligent care of the area to get to that point, you barely even notice it.

But then imagine you're making spaghetti carbonara (yum) over a gas stove, or maybe roasting a Juicy Jumbo hot dog over a campfire (YUM), and suddenly that old wound on your arm is closer than it has been in a while to a heat source, and bam!—there is a stinging pain that comes from how sensitive that scar tissue is to the pressure and the heat of the flame.

Our emotional scar tissue is like that too.

Thirteenth-century poet Rumi said that "your task is not to seek for love, but merely to seek and find all the barriers within yourself that you have built against it." Making peace with your emotional scar tissue goes a long way in finding those internal barriers you've built at every stop along the way.

If you imagine that the Self is composed of many, many selves, you can wrap your head around the notion that it's possible to heal one self, and then another, and then another, all from the ripple effects of the same wound. Yet still, when we're exposed to some kind of intense heat or pressure, that old wound is triggered and the scar tissue is sensitive again.

This is not a sign of failure.
Repeat: This is not a sign of failure.

It's not even a sign of being damaged or broken. It's actually excellent feedback that you've healed so beautifully well that you've made it safe enough to experience next-level healing of the same wound for other aspects of your Self.

Because our feelings are always feedback, each one offering incredibly valuable insights as to what still needs to be healed.

All this to say, here's what I know:
I am single.
Very, very single.
And while that means that technically I am alone, I am by no means *actually* alone, or even lonely . . .

. . . *because* I *am always with me.*

And if I am always with me, then *you* are always with *you.*
And if *I'm* never really alone, and *you're* never really alone, and we're not even alone in feeling like we *might* be alone, this conversation is one that needs to be had.

Which is why I wrote this book for you, specifically.

One of my specialties is understanding how our mind and our emotional body work together to process and heal; each of us is having a wildly similar and shared emotional experience here in Earth School for Humans, even if our physical life experiences present themselves differently.

And I know that if these feelings versus reality of what alone does and does not look like, I know there is someone, and very likely *many* some-ones, who need to know in black and white that they are not alone in the discomfort or the isolation of their emotional experience. That the emotional weight they've been carrying, largely in silence or maybe in self-deprecating humor, is no longer theirs alone to carry.

I have an extremely rich connection with the divine and have experienced firsthand many times over that we are always in the right place at the right time, and that life is constantly unfolding in the way that serves us best (and I bet you have too), AND STILL I sometimes feel absolutely overwhelmed by waves of grief for my single status.

I know I am not alone in that grief—and neither are you.

That's a big motivator behind this book: to share the comfort that comes from the insight of knowing you are not alone, even in your feelings, and that you are, in fact, in incredible company in what is weighing on your head and heart.

It's not just the alone-ness that comes from being *single*: it's the alone-ness that comes from the very human experience of living an authentic, purpose-driven, and intentional life.

When this book was just an idea for a book and not yet a *book* book, I shared the overview of my idea with my publisher, and she, a happily married woman, immediately expressed that she, too, has felt that same sting of "alone" in entrepreneurship (oof), in motherhood (double oof), and now in life, some eight thousand months into this stupid pandemic (all of the OOF!).

Which is why I know I had to, even if I didn't really want to, write this book.

I wrote *To Call Myself Beloved* because when I was learning how to go from self-loathe to self-love, I couldn't find the specific resource I needed to teach me HOW to fucking love myself. And in the past 38,000 days I have been single, give or take, I have just not been able to find THE resource I've been looking for to teach me *how* to be single when I don't want to be. And I definitely have not found one for "how to be alone."

I haven't been able to find the one guide that makes me feel seen and heard and comforted and like maybe it's okay to feel fucking great about being single one day, super trusting of the process and timing the next, and in a heap of tissue and pizza soon after that because this reality is what the human experience is like: hard.

I've often screamed out loud, "I don't know how to do this!!!" And one night, after the launch of my first best seller and the creation of my six-figure business and beating cancer and raising amazing kids and buying, then renovating a home on my own, I allowed myself the grace to finish what I *didn't know* was simply an incomplete sentence:

I don't know how to do this . . . and still, I am doing this.

And I think that is an excellent place to start.

PART ONE: CLARITY

CHAPTER ONE

I DON'T KNOW HOW TO DO THIS . . .
. . . AND STILL, I AM DOING THIS

"Being a kid is hard," my girlies told me one day. They were only about five and seven when we first had this conversation, standing in our cozy little kitchen by the sink, and at first, I thought they were teasing me.

So, I stopped and listened with a little more presence. I asked, "What do you find hard about being a kid?" As a single, self-employed, cancer-surviving solo parent of three, I knew *very well* what was hard about being a grown-up, and they really piqued my curiosity because from where I stood, being a kid (with a great and loving mom) was pretty sweet.

They told me how frustrating it is to have someone else decide what you can and can't eat and how much TV (and which shows) you can and can't watch, that it's frustrating splitting time between two houses and following two different parenting styles and being told what time you have to go to bed and how much you can and cannot read when you get there . . .

In our home, we have a pretty democratic family lifestyle in which my kids each have their own voice at the table and are encouraged to use it; they are included in decision making of weekly meal planning and how we spend our weekends and family vacations. And when they give feedback about what feels good and what doesn't, I listen, and we work together to figure out what does feel good for each of us as individuals and as a family.

To hear them communicate what effectively feels like their own limited freedom was so interesting to hear. And they were right: Being a kid *is* hard. They live with the freedom of having little responsibility and the burden of having little agency. They navigate friendship stuff and figure out emerging social technologies in real time without any of the experiential context of "what could go wrong," and they feel stuck somewhere in the middle.

Then I got thinking about how being a kid is hard, being a teen is hard, being a twenty-something is hard, being in your thirties is hard, growing old is hard . . . it's all hard.

Life is hard. Right?
It's *hard*.
We are constantly finding ways to deal with the hard-ness of it, from the time we're born until, I suppose, the time we die.

At every step along the way in between, we look for resources to comfort and make sense of this human experience. Or sometimes we look for things to just numb it out, and we keep going until we find the thing that works for us.

In my experience? It can even be hard to find *the* thing that works for us.

Therapy is good, coaching is good, earned and learned wisdom is good, tapping into pleasure and joy is good. And sometimes, while we're looking for and finding the good, it can feel like it's not quite enough, like it doesn't go deep enough, or isn't specific enough, or doesn't give us the complete context or skill set to make it enough.

Out of the myriad of things we can't control in our lives, there is one constant over which we always, *always* have agency: how we choose to react and respond to any given situation or circumstance in our life.

Often, the prescription for how you can do that is to:

- get to know yourself
- love yourself
- spend time with yourself
- care for yourself
- accept yourself
- trust the process
- surrender and let go

All of this *is* good.

And it *is* true.

And . . .

. . . it's usually not enough.

Why?

Because our brains are incredibly simple and incredibly complex, all at the same time.

My favorite analogy to describe how our brain works is to imagine a sheet of freshly fallen snow. When we're little, it's like we're just running around in this fresh and light, fluffy snow, leaving little pathways of footprints in the snow behind us without even thinking about it. It's effortless. And then, around age six or seven, it's as if there's a flash freeze that etches those pathways into ice.

Our brain likes status quo, which is to say that it *loves* things the way they are. It loves the status quo *so much*, in fact, that it will do whatever it takes to get you to follow the exact same pathways over and over and over and over and over and over and over again.

Because that is what feels safe.

Neurological and emotional safety is the core of literally *everything* we do, and nine times out of ten, when we find "the thing" that feels kinda good but doesn't feel like it's really enough? It's because it doesn't address our need, like our actual *need*, to maintain that level of internal and core safety.

Neurological safety is created in those early years of forming pathways: whatever paths we make in the "snow" of our brain (for example, the patterns we observe in our early days as to what love, partnership, belonging, acceptance, tenderness, intimacy, and attachment looks like) are what become our own unique baselines of reality.

As these baselines are forming, our subconscious mind is acting as our own built-in security guard, constantly scanning our environment for clues that we are safe and alerting us when we are in danger. When our subconscious perceives something as danger, or as a threat, it sends out chemical signals that we experience as a physiological fear signal—we are chemically shifted into flight, fight, freeze, or fawn mode.

Whenever our subconscious sweeps the environment and finds something that even remotely challenges status quo, i.e., something that is different than what we've already experienced and now "know" to be true, we are alerted to either rage up and fight, get the fuck out of there, become temporarily paralyzed, or do whatever it takes to make everyone else around us happy as a means of diffusing the (often emotional) threat.

So, back to the plain-truth reality that life is hard and that we are almost always looking for ways to make it easier (because our brain is also an inherent pleasure seeker and prefers things that feel easy because easy feels *good*), when we find advice that tells us to "just love ourselves," the reason it doesn't usually work is because "just loving yourself" is very likely in opposition to those early baseline patterns of neurological and emotional safety that we've been working to maintain behind the scenes for thirty, forty, fifty, eighty years.

If "loving yourself" goes against all the wiring and baseline patterning you're accustomed to, then before you can love yourself, you have to *teach* your brain that *it is safe* to love yourself.

And in the instance of being alone, while there may be some well-intentioned advice out there to just accept it, get to know yourself, trust the process, and let go, for many people, that isn't yet a reality because it doesn't yet feel *safe* to trust, surrender, accept, or let go.

That means that again, for a lot of us, learning to *be* alone is going to require some serious introspection and very likely guided mentorship through the process of subconsciously rewiring your brain to a place in which it *can* feel safe enough to *be* alone.

I've had a lot of therapy.
I've had a lot of coaching.

And I am here to tell you that there are *very few* healing practitioners who offer this subconscious deep dive as a part of their services. Very few. While most (certainly from my studious observations—and sure, on occasion, judgments) of what is available on the market in terms of self-development is practitioners focusing on the conscious work (talk therapy, goal setting, visualization, manifesting, etc.), the irony is that *most* of the deep and healing and long-lasting change comes from deep subconscious healing work.

It's like 90 percent of the self-help industry is focused on the 10 percent of the iceberg you can see; it ignores the other 90 percent of the iceberg you *can't* see. But when you ignore that 90 percent—the deep subconscious stuff that allows you to be clear on your values, core beliefs, previously held limiting stories or narratives, false thresholds of love/ success/intimacy/worthiness, then integrate them (or not) in a holistic and aligned way—you *will keep feeling* the not-enoughness.

Why does this matter?

Other than the fact that there's now a *bazillion-dollar* industry set up to sell lists and courses and one-size-fits-all programs that game and codify "healing" in a way that ignores *literally 90 percent of the stuff that needs to be healed* in order to experience real change?

It opens the door to having much more self-compassion.
We can choose to live as both/and in a world that asks us to pick either/or.

Understanding that we are simultaneously a divinely orchestrated work of art *and* a divinely orchestrated work in progress *is* what allows us to take a minute and appreciate that we're not going to get it right all the time. Hell, we're not going to get it right *most* of the time. And when you can wrap your head around that hard truth, soft pillow, it becomes a little more obvious that of course we don't know what we're doing. And still?

We are doing it.

Everything in this life, including the complex simplicity of *be*ing alone, takes time to learn and then perfect. In addition to healing from our own life experiences, many of us are healing generational—and yes, even past-life—wounding *while* figuring out how to carve out a career path, raise a family, care for parents, mow the lawn, navigate social media, make time for sex, tweeze, feed the dog, drink 2L of (collagen-infused) water, walk 10,000 steps, cut back dairy and caffeine, and catch up on eight seasons of *The Voice*.

It's a lot.

Giving yourself the grace to acknowledge and say out loud, "I don't know how to do this, and still, I am doing it" is this subtle but powerful statement to appreciate you are *in* this right now. You are *living* this. You are coming home to *know* yourself and trust that person again, or maybe for the first time.

And interestingly, pausing to give yourself that grace tenderly and lovingly helps to soften even our hardest emotional exterior and starts to forge a new sense of emotional and neurological safety in a way that *most* of us have not experienced before.

There's no right way, there's no wrong way, there's just your *way.*

I don't know how to do this, and still, I am doing this.
You don't know how to do this, and still, you are doing this.
No one anywhere knows how to do this, and still, everyone everywhere is doing this.

We're all just figuring this out, fumbling around in the dark, quietly blowing it when we get it wrong and silently celebrating when we get it right, learning how to come home to ourselves, where we belong.

Because when you belong to yourself, the truth and beauty of it is that you are never really alone.

CHAPTER TWO

HARD TRUTH, SOFT PILLOW

A few years ago, I found out that a *close* friend of mine had hosted a party and invited my ex-husband, but not me. And it hurt, to say the least. It hurt a lot.

"Not being chosen" was, for a painfully long time, the narrative leftover from my own parental estrangement at a startlingly early age that I had on infinity loop in my child and adult life, and here it was, being triggered again.

I remember finding out about the party and being so upset. I felt incredibly hurt that a "friend" of mine had had a party that she not only did not invite me to but invited my ex-husband instead, even after knowing many of the details of the very painful divorce of which we were in the middle.

I called my aunt, feeling rejected, excluded, cast aside, hurt, and really sad.

After explaining all the details, I communicated just how hurt my feelings were to have been completely left out of a party thrown by someone who just a few weeks earlier I'd taken on a girls' getaway weekend to the bougie-est hotel overlooking the lake in one of the nicest retreat spaces in the entire province of Ontario.

I just could not wrap my head around why I was left out, or how it was possible she didn't invite me, or what it was about my friendship that wasn't enough to be included (in a stupid keg party that frankly, I didn't even really want to be at). It was the principle, the lack of loyalty, and the triggering feeling of "you're not chosen, again" of it all.

My aunt, very warmly, gently, and matter-of-factly said, "Well, maybe she just likes him more than she likes you."

Oof.
Hard truth, soft pillow:
Maybe this friend person just didn't like me.

And in that moment of truth, without looking for other (untrue) explanations or justifications, I felt free. Empowered. Safe to accept the difficult reality that she *just didn't like* me as much as she liked my ex, which empowered me to take a good hard look at the people I was surrounding myself with and ask why the hell I would invest any amount of time, energy, or emotion in someone who did not give a shit about me.

And although that is a little harsh, the realization that she didn't really give a shit about me, it kinda felt like it transported me to this new reality in which *I didn't have to overthink or do an emotional postmortem* of what went wrong where and why or what I could have done "better."

I just . . . moved on.

And I moved on with wayyyyy better boundaries and more clearly defined expectations that align my values of a mutually respectful and nurturing friendship versus trapping myself in codependent relationships for fear of being alone.

This hard truth was so freeing, which is why I say very matter-of-factly and with so much nurturing warmth this ultimate hard truth with a soft pillow that is one of the cornerstone takeaways of this book:

You are going to die alone.

Oof, there it is.

It's like being hit with a hard truth as a soft pillow because that is life, and that is the level of wisdom I want to share with you in the honest guidance and mentorship you've been looking for to process your feelings rather than giving you a couple hundred pages of platitudes that leave you feeling inspired for ten minutes, then depleted when the high wears off.

You are going to die alone, and so am I.
So is everyone you know well and wish you didn't, and everyone you don't know well and wish you did.

All of us. The whole lot.
We're all going to die.
Alone.

Death, just like birth, is a solitary experience. Even if you are surrounded by people when you pass, ultimately, the act of passing itself is a solo passage to demarcate this life experience to . . . the next one.

We are, in large part, terrified of dying. We isolate sickness, death, and dying to sterile and poorly lit corridors with hand sanitizer at every threshold and the universal smell of "hospital." We keep the whole process at arm's length so as to avoid it for as long as possible.

We tell our kids things like "don't worry, that will never happen to me," and we romanticize growing old with someone, not fully appreciating the minutia and daily life reality that the "growing old" process entails mostly the decay of our physical and mental bodies.

Death is the ugliest truth of the beautiful illusion we call "life."

It's one of the best-kept secrets of our human experience. And when we keep something a secret, we keep it unknown, and when we keep it unknown, we necessarily make it feel like an absolute threat to our brain, which, as you know, is designed to stick to what we *do* know as a means of keeping us safe.

They say (*they* being the two old guys in the balcony of *The Muppets*) that there are two things in life you can depend on: death and taxes.

And if you start paying attention to even the smallest of towns you pass through, there is always an accountant, a Chinese restaurant, and a funeral parlor.

Thus, only a few things are certain:
- If you are born into life . . .
- . . . you will die.
- You will have some snacks along the way.
- You will have to pay tax on those snacks.

And yet, we tend to resist normalizing death as a truncated bookend to our own cycle of life.

What does all this have to do with being alone? Or with belonging?

Well, that fear of death is real because we are genetically predisposed to live.

And that fear of dying alone is real because we've established a false narrative that dying alone = failure, and so we compound our fear of physical death *and* social death (being rejected) into one superstorm that adds layers and layers of fear-motivated behaviors to do what it takes to feel loved so that we don't feel alone.

If/when we can consciously flip the script on and reframe the *inevitability* of dying alone (because again, the act of death is a *solitary* process), we can conceptualize the normalization of our own passing and then start to accept it as fact, and that acceptance can become a highly valuable and empowering tool to reframe our own fears of being alone period, thus allowing us to invest more wholly in belonging to ourselves.

Because when you belong to yourself, the truth and beauty of it is that you are never really alone.

CHAPTER THREE

WHAT IF THE END IS REALLY THE BEGINNING?

All three of my children were born naturally, without meds, in very peaceful labor and deliveries, including my twins. It was miraculous.

My first baby was born at home, which was an unparalleled moment of celebration in my life. The lights were dimmed, the house was quiet and cozy, I didn't know I was in labor for most of the night until I woke my then-husband a few hours in to say I was having the worst indigestion (and diarrhea) of my life, and he looked at me bleary-eyed and said, "Uh, I think you might actually be in labor."

He called our midwives, and the first arrived and began comforting me in my upstairs bathroom, saying not to worry because this was my firstborn and that we probably had lots of ti—
Oh my GOD, call the second midwife and tell her to get here immediately!

Turns out, I was not only in advanced labor, but this baby was coming. Like now.

We went into our guestroom, I sat on the little birthing stool, leaned against my then-husband, told my midwife there was no way in fucking hell I could do it, gave a push, and . . . wow!

She was born.
It was a superlative experience.

I had been intentional about naming, speaking with, and singing to each of my babies while they were in my belly, so the arrival of my firstborn into this physical world that we would now share together felt more like reuniting with a dear loved one I just hadn't seen in a long time.

Chills.

I remember my midwife (the second one never arrived, as it all happened too fast) handing me this tiny, precious human, and *I remember* her *looking around the room and blinking* as if she were taking it all in to get her bearings. It was as if she were just getting a sense of reorienting to which context she'd been brought into, figuring out what felt familiar and what felt new.

In that moment, I was 100 percent consciously and intuitively aware that *this little baby had done this before,* and she was just getting a sense of where she was now.

It was an *insane* feeling to witness this moment occur, and I can still flash back to it clearly as if it were happening again right in front of me now.

Chills.

In that moment it was as if one singular second in time had been paused, slowed, and stretched out *Matrix* style, just long enough for me to bear witness to this *remarkable* observation of adaptation, then radically sped up to play catch-up, only to return to the normal pace of life and mother-daughter bonding.

That moment is indelibly etched into my psyche.
She has done this before.

At that point in time, I was not the least bit "tuned in" to my own spirituality or "the Universe," manifesting, Law of Attraction, past lives . . . none of these were on my radar, nor had "woo woo" hit the widely accepted pop culture status it has today. God felt, at that point, like a four-letter word that I'd been taught to shame and dismiss throughout my upbringing, and having faith in myself—let alone faith in something bigger than myself—felt taboo, strange, and scary.

So, to effectively bear witness to this beautiful *soul* in the form of a tiny, precious, strawberry-blonde baby doing a quick environmental scan and recalibrating for what she was coming into blew open the door to an entirely new world I'd never even considered to be real.

In hindsight, after a lot of years, a lot of inner work, and a lot of coming home to myself and believing fervently in the divinity of alllll of this human experience, this moment really stands out in terms of knowing that *we don't know what we don't know.* For me, it felt like a glimmer of what happens when we transition from one life into the next.

Is this too weird?
Well, buckle up because it's about to get weirder. LOL.

When my second and third children (born four minutes apart) were about age four or five, we were chatting in their room before bed in the cozy little cottage house we rented just before I bought our family home. I don't remember the context of what we were talking about, but I *do* remember them saying, "That's why we chose you."

Uh . . . pardon?

"That's why we chose *you*; we were up there floating around, saw you and said, 'Well, that looks like a nice lady, let's choose her to be our mom.' And we zoomed down."

Chills.
This was a real conversation.

I remember being pregnant and reading that from the viewpoint of a particular Eastern culture, there was a belief that the Soul arrives in the body at five months gestation, and at that time, these people would throw a soul-welcoming party.

In the Western world, this time period is almost exactly when we can go in for the twenty-week scan where the assigned gender of this physical little body is revealed.

On top of that, in a moment of vulnerable transparency with my first midwife, I remember openly communicating my fears of being a parent for the first time. Very knowingly, the midwife said to me, "We choose the parents we need. I have seen that happen over and over again," which, coming from a seasoned midwife who'd already practiced twenty-plus years as a NICU nurse in South Africa, carried a lot of weight.

So, when my twinsies communicated this moment of "choosing" me, my midwife's comment was all that came to mind. My twins didn't become my daughters by accident; their souls *purposefully and specifically chose my soul* to be their mom and ultimately, their guide and facilitator of this particular lifetime.

Wild, right?

Sometimes I think that life is like a video game. Now, because I've literally only ever played *Tetris, Frogger, Snakebyte*, the OG *Super Mario* on the first iteration of Nintendo (the one that came mid-nineties standard with *Duck Hunt*) and a very brief stint with *NBA Jam* while on a ski vacation during March Madness, it's important to point out that my "video game" knowledge is rudimentary at best.

But still.

Think back to the OG *Super Mario* so many of us grew up with at our friend's place after school:

There you are, zipping along, living your life.
Really catchy music is playing, and you look so happy.
Every now and then, you jump up and hit a coin.
You feel *great*.

You're on your way to finding your friend, Princess Peach, when all of a sudden some crazy fucking turtle shell is launched at you.

You freak out.
You get knocked over.
You end.
You start again.

Now you see that GD turtle shell coming at you, and this time, baby, you're ready for it.
You've learned how to navigate the challenges on your path and to appreciate that it's only a challenging *moment*.
You learn to *anticipate* it. You jump the hell over it.
Hey, you did it!

You feel *really* great.
You feel so great that you get a super boost and now you jump higher than you knew possible, and after overcoming that hurdle (flying turtle shell), you hit like five coins in that power jump.

You get to the end of the level.

You feel . . . whole. Accomplished. Complete.

The screen goes dark . . .

. . . *and you find yourself in a brand-new level where you've never been before.* Yet, you're still able to use some of the lessons you learned in Level One, doing your best to apply them to each new challenge that comes your way in this brand-new, unknown Level Two.

I mean, you have to admit that there are a few similarities and overlaps here.

Think about when you were born, or even the concept of when you were born:

You're up there, tucked away in a cozy little womb where literally all of your needs are being met unconditionally. And then it's like the timer on the oven of your own divine timing is ready and you *know* instinctively it's time to end the cycle of being unborn in one environment only to begin the cycle of life in a brand-new (and incredibly unknown) environment.

Yes, you are born into the company of others, but still, this act of birth, this passage from one state of being to the next, is a remarkable solitary act.

I have this visual of that very special, unique, and solitary moment in which we are basically catapulted down the shoot from a dark and purple cosmic environment, hurtling toward some radiant field of light in which we are received into our next iteration.

While technically, our time in that dark and purple cosmic environment has come to an end, our time in this new and radiant, if entirely unknown, environment is just beginning.

Dude.
It's like the end is really the beginning.

So, if the "end" of our time in that little cosmic womb is really the beginning of our time in this human life, call me crazy, but it stands to reason that the end of *this* life is *really the beginning of our time in another life.*

Insert exploding head emoji here, right?

This conversation can take you down a deep, deep rabbit hole called "quantum physics," exploring beyond our 3D reality and moving into the 5D and even 12D realms to a place in which multiple timelines are not only possible but probable, quantum leaps are infinitely doable, and time is not only not linear, but basically nonexistent.

This world is beyond my pay grade (and clearly beyond my video game expertise), and I have to consciously moderate my engagement in exploring deeper concepts of quantum physics; it's so fucking fascinating that when I go down the rabbit hole, I can't physically concentrate on being able to bridge the gap of what could be true and what feels true, and I start to implode. It's like the best and most psychedelic trip . . . without ingesting any drugs or psychedelic plants.

But I can tell you that this claim is the absolute truth from my own very real and lived experience: The end of this life is absolutely the beginning of something else.

What the hell does any of this have to do with being alone or belonging? We're getting there; stay with me.

A few years ago, I had a series of surgeries that required anesthesia. During the second surgery, the one that removed my breasts in a radical mastectomy, I *vividly remember* seeing a light. Not a single beam of light, but an actual loving, warm aura of energetic light.

I also *vividly remember* being in conversation with a gentle voice, a warm energy that asked me if I wanted to "check out now."

Trust me, I could not make up this shit if I tried.

It was a very casual, grounded conversation in which I *vividly remember* the presence of this voice saying to me, "Are you sure? You can get off right here if you want. You could leave right now."

And I *vividly remember* being totally nonchalant about it and being unwavering in my answer of "no, I'm not ready to go yet; I'm not done, and I'd like to go back. I want to stay for a while." It was as casual and emotion free as if someone were asking me if I wanted to leave the party, and I was like "nah, I'm good. Let's grab a drink and chill here for a bit."

Duuuuuuuuuuuuude.

When I woke up from surgery, I felt calm and held. Grounded. Usually, me coming out of anesthesia is met with a lot of tears and emotion, but this time I just kind of felt *present.*

In the weeks, months, and years that have followed, this moment, juxtaposed with the moments of witnessing my firstborn's "recalibration" and my twins' recognition of *choosing* their dang mother, has given me much pause to think more deeply and far more abstractly about what it all means.

And at this point in time, what I believe "it" to all mean is that: *There. Is. A. Plan.*

The title of my first book comes from a tiny little four-line poem by Raymond Carver called "Late Fragment" that to me reads as a conversation between a woman at the "end" of her life and God: it reads like an exit interview, asking if she *did*, in fact, get everything she wanted out of this lifetime, which was simply to call herself beloved and feel herself loved back on the earth.

I think the reason this poem resonates so well and so deeply with me, to the extent that it's tattooed on the inner forearm of my right arm, is that to me, that adds up. It feels like each time before we come into a new iteration of our Self, our soul—which I believe is literally an infinite ball of energy that I can't even wrap my head around—sits down to make a plan as to what *specifically* it needs to learn in this lifetime.

I imagine it's our Soul, sitting down at some harvest table in the sky with a team of other beings, hashing out a plan, like they're writing a script of a movie, and the Soul is playing the leading role in that movie who also gets a writing and production cred in the end reel.

Far out, right?

In writing out that script, they know there needs to be drama.
There needs to be a great love story.
There needs to be action, foreshadowing, critical points of adversity, lots of B roll that we're not sure what we're going to do with yet, but we'll hang onto just in case, a bunch of laughs, poignant moments, and a killer soundtrack.

They're writing out the hero or heroine's journey.

I imagine them meticulously pouring over this script, editing as they go. "Are we sure about this plot line? It doesn't really seem fair. That guy seems like a royal asshole with a capital A. Cancer? Really? How does this all connect?"

"Yes. Think about it: How can she learn the lessons of deep self-love and acceptance and truly feeling whole on her own if she isn't faced with incredible challenges along the way that force her to choose real love?"

"Okay, good point. We better pepper in some really easy stuff too, so she doesn't just give up. Honey, can you handle this?"

"Will there be tacos? Laughs? Pleasure? Love and wonder? Yeah, I can handle it. Fuck it; let's do it."

Is this scenario a little *too* far out? Maybe, but to me? It is what makes the most sense, and through the throes of my own imagination of my life as a screenplay, here's what I'm getting at:

There is a plan.

We were a part of creating that plan.
We consented to that plan.
We are living that plan.
And when that plan is over, we'll go over and review what worked and what didn't quite get resolved, and we will use that information to create the next plan—the sequel to our own life story.

It does not mean it will be easy; it does not mean it will be comfortable; it sure as *hell* does not mean it will feel fair, or even make sense at the time. It means there is a *plan*, even when we can't see it or make sense of it right away, and everything that happens, for better and for worse, is a part of that plan. And if everything that happens is a part of that plan, then it also means going through the often dark, unsettled seasons in which we feel alone or that we don't belong is its own part of that plan.

And if all of that is planned, what it ultimately means is that you are truly never alone, unchosen, left out, or overlooked because you somehow made it here *with that divine orchestration* and thus, you are already in good company, chosen, included, and looked out for.

Hard truth, soft pillow?

You belong here.

And when you belong to yourself, the truth and beauty of it is that you are never really alone.

CHAPTER FOUR

ONE DEAD MONKEY

There was a documentary on Netflix a while ago called *Born in China*. One of my daughters wanted to watch it because it was about animal families; I wanted to watch it because John Krasinski is the narrator.

Win-win.

As is typical of animal documentaries, even the ones narrated by tall, handsome, understatedly confident, and funny men, there was a lot of cuteness and some really interesting facts marred by the trauma and painful reality of animal living.

It's not just the human experience that's hard, it's *existing on Earth* that's hard.

And considering in the grand schematic timeline of the universe that it wasn't that long ago that we ascended from primates, much like the ones featured in this documentary, it was pretty interesting to watch the relational dynamics play out in primate social and family groups and draw uncannily similar parallels to our own life.

For example, there's one part in which one little monkey just isn't as strong as the others in the troop; he doesn't come from an elite lineage, he doesn't have the physical or resourceful strength the others have to contribute in the same ways they do, and he really just needs some help meeting his basic needs so that he *can* learn to contribute like that.

Spoiler alert: The rest of the troop rejects him. And I mean *rejects* him. They openly shun him, throw rotten fruit at him, and even attack him when he gets too close or infringes on their own social and physical resources. And still, this tiny little monkey keeps going back, and back, and back, with what sure seems to be the intention of eventually being included, until his ultimate death. Oy.

It's painful to watch, and while it opened up a valuable conversation in our family of what it means for society to take care of *all* its members, it also illustrated the other painful reality that we are *driven* to belong as a part of the group, no matter what, at a deep biological and genetic level.

We are social creatures: We rely on acceptance *within* the group as our survival. Yes, we've evolved to meet many of our needs independent of the group. We source and gather our food at the grocery store, we hire contractors to build our shelter, we buy our clothes from The Gap, hell, we can even have our (collagen-infused) water delivered in a monthly subscription.

So much of our survival in the postmodern world is *beyond* the physical, and our conflicted relationship to the rotating lockdowns and social restrictions governments around the world served up as a response to navigating COVID-19 was a testament to that. What will the effects of the secondary pandemics of isolation and mental health be left in their wake? While we don't yet know the full extent to which it will affect "the after time," I bet you have your own share of personal experiences and predictions to draw from already.

The bottom line is that deeply embedded in our DNA, our species is programmed to equate *belonging* to the group as *safety*, both physical and emotional, and much of this feeling of safety includes connection and close, amicable social interaction, which is a fancy way of saying that for humans . . .
Rejection or the absence of love is perceived as the same as death.

Read. That. Again.

If we feel, or if our subconscious *perceives* us to feel separate from "the group," emotionally or physically, it literally feels like we are about to die; in the absence of either, we're basically one dead monkey.

Needless to say, these fears we have of "being alone" aka "not belonging" are real.

And it gets worse.

Back in the day, people only needed to belong to a relatively small number of people in their immediate family group, community, or tribe. These fears were real *even when* it was a fairly compact group people needed to be accepted by or belong to in order to soothe those fears of survival.

Fast-forward a few hundred years, smack dab in the middle of the Wild West of the internet and *several* social media platforms, our family, community, and social groups are literally thousands (if not tens or *hundreds of thousands*) of people we feel like we need to be accepted by or belong to for our survival. Despite the fact that most of these people exist to us *only* on the internet, and we'll likely *never* meet them in real life, like ever, it still *feels* like this is the group to which we must belong.

Our brains evolve at a *glacial* pace, meaning that while our human "software" can experience wild and exponential growth and evolution in the physical world, our human "hardware" evolves at a painfully slow pace, keeping a huge part of our brain anchored in primate-style patterns of needs-meeting behavior patterns.

Our need to belong to and be accepted by the group remains the same, but the group(s) that we feel compelled to belong to and accepted by have exploded in scope to the point that we have lost context of which group is even real, making us feel, ironically, much more isolated.

We live in a world where we've never been more connected, yet we've never felt more alone.

If we are constantly looking *outward* to the hundreds of thousands of people and lives we have access to in traditional and social media, we are constantly putting ourselves in a state of feeling threatened by what resources we don't have, which groups we don't belong to, and what we're missing out on. It's a state of perpetual lack and perpetual fear, and it is driven largely by economic strategies to keep us feeling less than and wanting more by capitalizing on our *primal fear* of not being accepted.

*casually deletes social media apps from phone

Remember the ViewMaster toy from when we were kids? You'd pop in a photo lens of say, the Muppets, click through and look at all your Muppet pals using the little orange lever on the side? You remember how you'd have to remove that lens if you wanted to see something *other than* the Muppets, like Fraggle Rock? Then, after you switched the lens and the Muppets were nowhere near your field of view, it was all Fraggle Rock, all the time?

Good news / bad news? Our brain is kind of like a ViewMaster, and our subconscious is the lens through which we look to see what we see and perceive what we perceive.

Because our brain *loves* status quo, and our subconscious *is designed* to warn us that anything in opposition to status quo is dangerous, the lens through which we look only allows us to see proof of what we already believe to be true, to be true.

It's like if I say to you, "Wow! There are so many black SUVs driving around today!" or "Whatever you do, don't think of a pink elephant," I'm willing to bet that you see more than the average number of black SUVs driving around than you're used to and that there's some weird-ass image of a pink elephant in your mind right now.

So, if you believe at a deep and subconscious level that men are assholes, relationships are really hard work, true love doesn't exist, and you can't make money doing what you love, chances are your little mental View-Master lens will continue to bring you examples of people, narratives, and situations that *all* confirm that to be true.

That's the bad news.

The good news is that like an actual ViewMaster, all you have to do is *change the lens* to change your entire perspective. Investing in someone who can help you do that at the subconscious level is an *invaluable* and life-changing experience because it changes the lens at your core, allowing you to see things completely differently. You'll see that there are wonderful men in the world, that healthy relationships are easy to navigate, and that true love not only exists but exists within your reach as does well-paying work that makes you feel *alive*. When you change that lens by changing your subconscious beliefs, you've shifted your own inner narrative, empowering yourself to look for proof plus confirm what you *now* know to be true.

Bam. You just rewired your brain in such a way that establishes a new baseline pattern of neurological and emotional safety, which means it will literally feel like a brand-new world or like you're seeing the world with brand-new eyes through your brand-new lens.

This shit is fucking magical.

How does that relate to being alone and feeling like you do or don't belong?

Our desire to connect with others is real, and when it's unrequited, it runs the risk of feeling quite *dis*connected, and that *dis*connection makes us feel not only not accepted by or belonging to but completely separate from the group, leading to painful feelings of isolation.

Knowing that we're kind of swimming upstream in fighting against our own biological and genetic programming of *needing* to belong, we can belay some of those primal fears by consciously putting ourselves in relationships and environments in which *we do* feel like we belong and are accepted.

And since we only ever have control over how we respond to something, a lot of this work is to

1. Dramatically shrink the size and scope of the context to which we even desire to belong, and
2. Reframe what it means to belong.

Even though the path of life we walk is effectively a solitary one of continually walking back home to our true self, the pressure to belong is huge and is supported by codependent patterns perpetuated by pop culture and media. And those pressure-building patterns are fueled by a multibillion-dollar budget called "advertising" and "Hollywood." You get to choose the scope and quality of content you interact with and consume. If the pressure feels too intense, you also get to choose to unfollow, delete, and swipe left on all the things that are designed to tell you that you'll never be enough on your own or as you are.

Period.

If you can't control your own glacially evolving neurobiology, then making peace with / accepting the fact that there may *always* be a part of you that is prone to feeling afraid of being left out or rejected is huge. By accepting that those feelings are not only natural but damn near *universal* to all humans on the planet, you can let go of the shame or self-judgment you have for being afraid of having a difficult conversation or otherwise being in emotional conflict, which is also *huge.*

We will very likely never lose or "overcome" our desire to connect; so, when that connection to yourself is unwaveringly strong, it suddenly becomes enough to belong to yourself. Wrapping your head around the sure-footed comfort that comes from belonging first and foremost to yourself is also, you guessed it, huge.

Because when you belong to yourself, the truth and beauty of it is that you are never really alone.

CHAPTER FIVE

FIGHT, FLIGHT, FREEZE . . . OR FAWN

I don't know about you, but I used "the bathroom" as an excuse to take a break from a lot of classes in high school. I seldomly *really* had to go, and I often *really* needed a break from Pythagoras and his theorem. I remember one day in tenth grade, I was walking just slowly enough down the smelly corridor so as to not draw attention from any incoming teachers or passersby as I meandered my way to the girls' room.

When I got there, I saw Crystal,[2] a renowned high school badass with a mean gaze and overall unpleasant demeanor, setting the garbage can on fire. She looked at me with her signature dead-eyed intensity and said, "You better not fuckin' tell."

---

2 To protect the privacy of the individuals discussed, all names in the book are pseudonyms.

I was pretty scared. Not only was the can full of paper towels *on fire*, but I'd witnessed firsthand what had happened, perpetrated by someone who gave me the evil chills in her very presence. Crystal left, and I, frozen in place for a minute, had to make a decision. And the decision I made?

Walk away.
I walked away. Calmly. Back to class. Past at least two fire alarms.

Did I pull them?
No.

Did I run back to class?
Also no.

I calmly went back to my math class, told my teacher there was a fire in the girls' room and that it was there before I got there, then pretended Crystal didn't even factor into it.

Why? Because I was scared.

In my twenties, I was walking along Queen Street West in Toronto with friends. We were in between bars and at a particularly sketchy intersection when a particularly sketchy woman came at me out of *nowhere*. Like nowhere. She just appeared in my face, screaming and looking like she was going to attack.

It took a minute for me to figure out that the other screaming I heard was my own due to the sudden appearance of this wild woman up in my space out of literally nowhere, and I was certain I was going to be assaulted in some way. As quickly as she appeared, she was knocked down on the ground by one of the guys walking with me. It all happened so fast.

He saw her get aggressive with me, and his instinct was to fight. He took her down and pinned her against the sidewalk while saying, "You stay down, you stay down!" until we all caught up to real time again and could safely part ways.

Why? Because he was scared.

An old friend told me the story of how, when she was a single woman, she was confident if anyone ever broke into her home that she'd rage up, get in their face and fight relentlessly. Years later, as a not-single woman, her teenage stepson came home unexpectedly while she was vacuuming and couldn't hear anything, and when she turned around, all she saw was a tall male figure, and she fainted, flat out.

Why? Because she was scared.

In those moments of our life when our physical safety is threatened, we get a surge of adrenaline as that one moment seems to stretch out and expand beyond what seems physically possible. People often describe time as slowing down while simultaneously happening super fast during those really threatening moments. And in those moments, our brains do a *wild* amount of assessment in order to figure out the danger and the appropriate response.

I bet you know what it feels like to be in those triggering moments of fight, flight, or freeze.

Each is a physiological response to fear and what our subconscious identifies as dangers or threats to our safety.

And there's another response that can be triggered as well, particularly if the threat our subconscious perceives to be dangerous is emotional: the fawn response. Pete Walker, psychotherapist and author of *Complex PTSD: From Surviving to Thriving*, coined the term "fawning" to refer to the response *many* people develop as children as a result of having emotionally neglectful or abusive parents. It, too, is a behavioral response to *trauma* that we have often called "people pleasing" or codependency, and it is rooted in our deep desire to do *whatever it fucking takes* to keep the peace and avoid further conflict at home.

Why? Because *we were scared.*

We know we are programmed to be a part of the group, and we know the basics of how our brain works to protect us from danger, i.e., not being a part of the group. But when that "group" is our parents, on whom we depend for our literal survival—physically as babies and emotionally as kids—then we feel incredibly threatened. I am by no means a psychologist, and still, one need not have a psych degree to draw the lines between needing to do *whatever it fucking takes* to feel loved and accepted by our parents to the often detrimental neglect of our own needs.

That means that for *many* of us, we learn at a very early age to repress our emotions in favor of toeing the line of what we think our parents expect of us. It's so damn toxic.

What's even more toxic is that while fawning *is* a trauma-related response to fear of emotional danger when we're little, it becomes our *baseline relational pattern* with respect to how we interact with others. In other words, "Let me do whatever it takes to meet your needs, to the detriment and repression of my own needs, all in an attempt for me to feel loved."

Oh shit, right?

I cannot tell you how often this specific conversation comes up in my one-on-one work with my private coaching and mentorship clients, all of whom, by the way, are accomplished high achievers (we're talking lawyers, high-level and often public-facing executives of multiple seven-figure companies, celebrities, authors, 1% realtors, PhD and post-doc grads, psychologists . . .) who learned at an early age to do *whatever it fucking takes* until they reached a breaking point (often in their forties, but not always) and realized that they have *no idea what they want*, they are afraid of wanting what they want and how to ask for it, and they feel depleted across the board from not getting their needs met.

Why? *Because they feel fucking scared.*

It's one of those beautiful flaws in our design: We develop this artificial coping mechanism that (and having *lived it* for approximately thirty-two years of my life, I can attest to) works. Until it doesn't.

And because the brain loves status quo, because the status quo is easy and easy feels good, when we try and confront or even break this relational pattern as an adult (in our work, family, friendships, partnerships, or all of the above), we are triggered by our subconscious to now fight, flee, or freeze as a response to implementing a new and healthy relational pattern centered around boundaries, getting our needs met, and open, loving communication.

It's so fascinating, and in a few chapters, we're going to explore how to begin the process of safely unlearning this pattern when it no longer serves us as a means to shift the attention to being able to safely identify what it is we want and need and how to safely draw those new boundaries with others by safely drawing them for ourselves first.

When you are safe to feel your feelings and openly know and then *trust* what you want and need, you deepen your connection to yourself and feel less of that achy *need* to get your needs met by someone else.

Being able to safely rely on yourself is fundamental to feeling like you belong to yourself.

And when you belong to yourself, the truth and beauty of it is that you are never really alone.

CHAPTER SIX

MONOPHOBIA

Recently, I have had two men offer to come and make dinner for me; naturally, I said yes to both of them.

The first arrived with a package of pasta and a package of frozen shrimp that came with a package of frozen sauce and a package of (not frozen) salad that came with a package of dressing. After I showed him how to navigate my gas stove, which he'd never used before, he heated the shrimp, heated the pasta, heated the sauce, then tossed it all together. He opened the salad to mix in its prepared dressing, but I could smell from across the room that the salad greens were *well* past their prime; playfully not believing me, he sniffed, s n i f f e d, then sniffed again, finally conceding that they were, in fact, inedible.

The second, to my delight, showed up with a box of fresh groceries and proceeded to smash garlic with his own Japanese blade, crumble sausage from our local butcher into a pan, pulse avocado and pesto into a food processor with lemon and parmesan until smooth, boil pasta, blister cherry tomatoes, toss it all together and plate it for me, all while he whisked ingredients into a dressing for butter lettuces, zested a lemon over my dish, oven toasted a ciabatta, and sat down with a yin-yang of oil and vinegar plate to go with said ciabatta.

Both of these (awesome) guys put dinner on the table for a lovely evening, but one knew how to make food . . . and one knew how to *cook*.

It's really, really easy to blend things together or overgeneralize with language, and it's really, *really* important that we are conscious about the language we use in conversations (with ourselves and others) because the words we use shape, inform, or reinforce existing patterns of language: When we give meaning to something, we give it power, so when we are conscious about what we're giving meaning to, we are actually being conscious about the context we're using to shape the world around us.

It is that simple; it is that complicated.

I told you earlier that my own fears of being single weren't really about being single—they were about the *alone-ness* of being single, which got me thinking, is there a word for *that*?

Turns out there is: *Monophobia* is defined as an actual fear or phobia of being alone or on one's own. Fear of being alone has a name, but it doesn't differentiate from fear of loneliness and is often interchanged with autophobia (ironically, not a fear of cars) and isolophobia, which is specific to fear of isolation (aka "Global Lockdown 2020").

And that got me thinking. It seems kind of important to be very clear on what we're talking about in a more definitive / less abstract way when we're talking about "being alone."

"Alone" isn't a dreaded four-letter word; there's a context in which we *make* it a dreaded four-letter word by assigning it a value / judging it for being a bad thing. In that context, we're giving it meaning.

For example, people spend *thousands* of dollars on alcohol and other numbing agents to dull the pain of being alone with their thoughts, and people spend *thousands* of dollars to go on multiday silent retreats just to be alone with their thoughts.

Alone technically means you are the only one there; it's the *intentionality* behind being alone that makes the difference.

When I was in high school, there was an ESL program that used our social studies classroom on the weekends. I remember walking into social studies one Monday morning, only to find our entire class covered with sticky notes:

Chair
Table
Map

Chalkboard

Overhead projector (because hey, it was the nineties and overhead projectors were a legit technology)

Literally every *thing* was labeled so that the students, brand new to the English language, could interact with and have agency over their environment by being fully confident in and aware of what each of the different parts was called. Naming those *things* suddenly *gave them meaning.*

This fact is true for all humans, in all environments—understanding what "stuff" is called is what allows us to participate in the conversation in an informed, intelligent way.

Well, guess what? The same is also true for our inner and emotional environment—understanding what stuff is called is what allows us to participate in the conversation in an informed, intelligent way.

The thing is, it's quite rare that we stop and think about the specific emotion we're feeling in favor of overgeneralizing and "chunking up" or lumping similar things together in a way that glosses over the specifics and the context. "I am so sad" versus "I am feeling despondent and longing from the pain of the loneliness I'm experiencing right now," for example.

Vague versus Specific.

"Pass me a writing implement" is a lot vaguer than "Pass me the black Sharpie with the fine tip" or "Pass me the purple pencil crayon."

"Let me make you dinner" is a lot vaguer than "Let me heat up a few packages of frozen food for you" or "Let me cook you rigatoni with local sausage, avocado pesto, and blistered cherry tomatoes with butter lettuces and oven-toasted ciabatta."

Philosopher Paul Tillich said, "Language . . . has created the word 'loneliness' to express the pain of being alone. And it has created the word 'solitude' to express the glory of being alone."

The words we use *matter*, yet very seldomly do we have the right words to describe what we're feeling, so we lump it all under one umbrella category like "sad" or "lonely," then try and treat that emotion, only to realize that our actions didn't work because we weren't being specific enough about what we were actually feeling.

So, let's just take a hot minute to define what the heck means what—all relate to the vague context of "being alone" and finding the truth and beauty of belonging—so that we can be crystal fucking clear on what we're talking about moving forward and how we specifically feel about each term.

Alone: having no one else present; to be on one's own, indicating that something is confined to the specified subject or recipient.

Lonely: feeling unhappy because you are not with other people.

Loneliness: the state of being lonely.

Solitude: the situation of being alone, often by choice.

Isolation: the condition of being separated from other people; the condition of being alone, especially when this state makes you feel unhappy.

Longing: a strong desire; the feeling of wanting something or someone very much.

Relationship: the state of being connected.

Connection: the act of joining or being joined to something else.

Boundaries: how emotionally or intimately close you allow people into your life; specific lines with respect to what is and is not acceptable in having a relationship with you.

Codependency: a behavior pattern in relationships in which you prioritize the needs of others, often at the expense or detriment of your own.

Emotional Alchemy: the term I coined for taking something dark, heavy, and unwanted and consciously transforming it into something light, beautiful, and uniquely your own. My first book walks you through this process step by step if you're looking for a reference.

Belonging: to be in the right or suitable place; to feel happy or comfortable in a situation.

And when you belong to yourself, the truth and beauty of it is that you are never really alone.

PART TWO: CONFIDENCE

CHAPTER SEVEN

NORMALIZING LONELINESS

I grew up in the eighties and nineties, back in the "golden age" of commercials, meaning streaming hadn't been invented yet, and Netflix didn't exist, so therefore, if we were watching TV, we were watching commercials.

I don't know about you, but every time I saw a soda (and eventually a beer) commercial, it was as if this magical algorithm of human behavior appeared:

1. Crack open a soda.
2. A DJ appears.
3. Beautiful people swarm your yard.

Or

1. Crack open a beer.
2. A DJ appears.
3. Beautiful people swarm your rooftop patio.

Or

1. Crack open an iced tea.
2. A DJ appears.
3. Beautiful people swarm your lake house, a pool appears, and you blissfully fall into it. But I digress.

I have cracked a lot of sodas in my life. There has been no DJ. No swarm of beautiful people.

The charcoal grill, hot-girl summer romance, and endless laughs with burly men I was promised by *so many* commercials of my youth just did not happen.

I tried it with beers, iced tea, champagne, bourbon, tequila, and whiskey for good measure, and I can assure you that in each and every instance, while sugar and alcohol dependency *certainly* made a guest appearance, a DJ, a pool, and a giant group of beautiful friends did not arrive.

It doesn't work like that because life isn't a soda commercial.
Life can feel pretty lonely sometimes.
Life can actually feel *very* lonely, even.

Loneliness is such a heavy emotion that it can be hard to process, and just like any "negative" or heavy emotion, when it feels hard to process, we tend to repress it, bypass it, and keep it to ourselves, all three of which add an even heavier layer—like a wet blanket—of shame on top that feels like "I shouldn't even be feeling like this / I can't feel like this / look at my life; how could I be lonely / nobody else feels like this / I am such a failure / I can't tell anyone about how I feel.

Understanding that our feelings are just feedback offering valuable insights as to what still needs to be healed and that you have to, *have to* feel it to heal it, then we come to realize that repressing, bypassing, and isolating won't lift the loneliness, they exacerbate it.

Here's a hard truth, soft pillow: Everyone feels lonely sometimes. Everyone feels alone in their loneliness.

Very few people feel comfortable admitting to themselves, let alone to someone else, that they feel lonely because admitting it feels like alerting the brain to danger of rejection, which, as we know, feels like death (i.e., if I feel lonely, I mustn't be loved, and if I am not loved, I am dead).

One of the best kept secrets of our species, though?
Part of the human condition is to feel lonely, ironically making it a shared human experience, just one that we rarely share openly.

It starts with your physical separation from anything else:
Your one body is a complete system that is independent of any other physical body or thing, meaning that you are physically alone. Even your thoughts are separate from anyone else's thoughts. You may know what *you* are thinking, and you can listen to and then interpret what someone else is thinking, but you will never know with certainty what they're really thinking, thus, technically, everyone is mentally and emotionally alone.

From Aristotle to Nabokov, Balzac to Nietzsche, Picasso to Gandhi, philosophers, leaders, artists, and writers have been studying loneliness and its relationship to the human condition for longer than you and I have been alive, and they will continue to do so long after we're gone. Knowing that we are simultaneously alone and paradoxically never alone is an endless source of content worthy of exploring.

Thomas Wolfe said, "Loneliness . . . is the central and inevitable fact of human existence. When we examine the moments, acts, and statements of all kinds of people—not only the grief and ecstasy of the greatest poets but also the huge unhappiness of the average soul . . . we find, I think, that they are all suffering from the same thing. The final cause of their complaint is loneliness."

Well, guess what? These really smart folks didn't corner the market on exploring loneliness—teams of really smart folks at advertising agency headquarters and marketing departments across the globe joined the bandwagon to *exploit* that loneliness. Ultimately, commerce and capitalism work so well because they embody the Vanilla Ice approach to life: Is there a problem? Yo—we'll solve it.

When there's a problem, *teams* of people sit down to hash out a solution via a product that can be sold to you. And thank goodness. Food gets stuck in your teeth? Bam, here's some dental floss.
Problem melts away with the solution.

The big issue with this problem solving is that in knowing what we know about the human condition, our desire for certainty, and our inherent knowing that life is finite while also denying that reality for as long as possible, these teams of really smart folks have started selling solutions to problems that either don't exist or that can't be solved.

And they've built a bazillion-dollar industry in doing so.

As soon as there is a glimmer of a gap in the market or in human desire with the perception that it could be filled, you can be certain there'll be a team of ad execs available to fill that gap by telling a story on behalf of their client about how this one thing—usually low in its investment of time and money so as to reach as many of the seven billion people on the earth as possible—will make that problem go away.

They don't even have to say, "We know you're feeling lonely," they just have to give you the whisper of hope that on a regular Saturday afternoon by yourself, all you have to do is crack open that soda and that loneliness you're feeling will go away.

So, we crack the soda, the people don't appear, and we still feel lonely. In fact, we probably feel *lonelier still* because hey, if this is the thing that works for everyone else, now we have "conscious proof" from what we've seen on TV that we really are a loser destined for a lifetime of eternal loneliness . . . unless . . . wait, are those the new Jordans? Maybe if I get those, I'll feel like I'm a part of something.

You see the slippery slope here, right?

Add the fact that TV and movies are bazillion-dollar industries that thrive when viewership and ratings are high (so they can sell valuable ad space for soda, weight loss, and antidepressants), so they create storylines around what the execs think will drive ratings. Therefore, if they already know we tend to feel lonely (which is a normal part of the human experience), they show back-to-back shows about fictional friends and families who literally never feel the normal feeling of loneliness, then, at the commercial break, they sell something that gives the illusion that this thing is *the* missing piece that can bridge the gap from feeling lonely to feeling like you belong . . .

Then just like that, they sold you the problem *and* the solution in twenty-two minutes or less.

I am *hypergeneralizing* here, but you get the point: There is an industry built from programming us to believe one thing so that we are fear motivated into buying the things that those same conglomerate companies sell to "make us feel better."

Alcohol. Cigarettes. Micro doses of drugs. Gambling. Sex. Overspending. Bigger versions of the things you already have. All the things that have seriously addictive side effects are being constantly sold as the solution to your problems. It's all fueled by the rhetoric that THIS WILL MAKE YOU LESS LONELY! THIS WILL MAKE YOU HAPPY!

And it's not true because, to quote Poppy from *Trolls*, "Happiness isn't something you *put* inside; it's already there." Companies that both create and capitalize on the problem they're selling the solution to don't want you to know it, but once you know, and I mean *really know*, it's a bell you can't unring.

So, what if we reframe it from "WTF is wrong with me and what can I DO about it" to "Hey look, I'm having a normal human feeling; how can I cultivate my ability to make *peace* with it and feel supported in doing so?"

No, it's not necessarily comfortable, but neither is going to the dentist or getting a pap, yet somehow, we've found a way of normalizing those necessary appointments as a part of our overall health plan.

Knowing that:
1. There is a plan, and
2. We are each walking our own path, and
3. Part of the human condition is to feel "separate" from others while simultaneously deeply desiring intimacy and connection
    . . . we can start to flip the switch on "loneliness" and start accepting the fact—*the fact*—that loneliness is a part of our experience in all areas of our life.

Accepting and then embodying that very human reality might not make loneliness any more comfortable, but what it *does* do is it puts you back in the driver's seat of your own emotions and brings back the empowering element of choice: If loneliness is just a part of "all this," then loneliness can be reframed as a normal human emotion that literally everyone feels.

And if loneliness can be reframed as a normal human emotion that literally everyone feels, you have the choice as to what you do with that feeling: You can judge it as bad, let it wash over you and make you feel like you're drowning, or you can be real with your feelings that "this is what loneliness feels like" and find your own unique way to use Emotional Alchemy to make that feeling, and the experience of that feeling, your own. In a bit, we're going to explore some really practical ways you can do this process for *you*, and in doing so, take back your own power, even during those really icky, uncomfortable, pizza-laden, and sometimes downright *painful* feelings.

That is the shit that feels so good.
That is the shit that deepens your connection to and relationship with yourself.
That is the shit that makes you feel like you *belong*.

Because when you belong to yourself, the truth and beauty of it is that you are never really alone.

CHAPTER EIGHT

THE MYTH OF UNCONDITIONAL LOVE

"In the end, we all just want someone who chooses us, over everyone else, under any circumstances." How many times have you seen this meme floating around your social platforms? I was confident that it was a Shonda Rhimes original from the early seasons of *Grey's Anatomy* (can't you just hear Meredith Grey saying these words in voiceover as the camera pans in on poignant moments unfolding in Seattle Grace and nearby luxury condos as Tegan and Sara or Snow Patrol play wistfully in the background?), BUT it turns out it's one of those viral memes that everybody shares and nobody knows where it came from or who wrote it.

If you *do* know, tell me; I'd like to sit down and dig into the myth of unconditional love with them. Wanting someone to choose you over everyone else and under any circumstance is wanting the kind of love that has no boundaries, no conditions, and is frankly rife with codependency and very likely enmeshment slash super unhealthy obsession.

It's okay to be a hopeful romantic and still loathe shit that sounds good and Instagrammy on the surface but unconsciously perpetuates a message that sets people up for widely unrealistic, unhealthy, unrequited expectations over and over again.

Hard truth, soft pillow?
Unconditional love is incredibly rare.

Think about it: to love or be loved by someone *no matter what* and *in any circumstance*.
No matter what someone does, you love them anyway.

It doesn't usually work like that, and if it *does* work like that, I'd strongly recommend sitting down with a pro to explore some patterns of behavioral codependency that might be factoring in.

In any relationship, not just with an intimate partner, the ideal dynamic is a Venn diagram:

Unhealthy: Two people who "divide and conquer" and are completely separate.

Unhealthy: Two people who lose their individual sense of self to codependency or enmeshment.

Healthy: Two independent people living an interdependent life, each keeping a sense of self while being in partnership with another.

Two independent people living an interdependent life, each keeping their own unique sense of self while being in partnership with another. The interdependency is the shared relationship they have, while they still remain very much their own independent being.

This healthy relationship model is true for client/professional, child/ parent, friend/friend, sister/sister-in-law, person/money, and *definitely* partner/partner.

Healthy, loving relationships function from a place of healthy, loving boundaries. And those boundaries are communicated in a healthy, loving way.

The trouble with looking for, anticipating, or expecting unconditional love from another is that it literally sets you up to fail. Think about it: We are built to survive. And we are built to love. But if our need to survive is threatened by someone else—even if we love them, and even if we *really* love them—we inherently choose our own survival.

"Yeah, but what about our kids?"

As a parent I wrestle with this question, especially in the writing of this chapter, because of all the people and relationships in my life, I can say with 100 percent accuracy that I love my kids unconditionally. My love for them is steadfast, based on nothing other than I love and accept them for who they are. And I bet it's the same for you.

Unless . . . what if . . . your kid did something truly heinous? Like what if they committed a heinous act that hurt another one of your kids? Would you love and accept them then? This question is a dark one, I know, and the answer is still probably a yes, and the only reason I'm bringing it up is to illustrate that it's easy to talk about unconditional love, but when we start to explore what it means—to love someone over anyone else, in any circumstance—it kind of sounds crazy.

"Well, what about my kids loving *me* unconditionally? I mean, I *am* their parent, after all."
This relationship is a fallacy as well.

Hard truth, soft pillow? Most of us have a tipping point in the love we have with our parents too.

Wow, this got dark fast. But think about it: Can you honestly say that you love your parents, no matter what, under any circumstance? Probably not.

Culturally, we tend to fetishize parental relationships to be this unbreakable bond, full of loving mentorship and supportive wisdom. From my own life, and from my front-row seat into the lives of others in my coaching and mentorship practice, I can tell you with 100 percent certainty that it is a myth.

It absolutely exists for some people, but the idyllic parent–child bond we wish and deserve to have, as both the child and the parent, is a reality for *some* people, and is sadly *not* the norm.

The truth is that most—*most*—people have an incredibly tortured relationship with their parents and have grown up and lived in such messed-up/bizarre/toxic/abusive relationships that they've had to, out of emotional survival, normalize the threshold of what love looks and feels like.

And then they spend thirty years in therapy overcoming it.
Prove me wrong.

Using the metaphor that each of us is an individual walking our own path alongside seven billion other individuals walking their own path, parenting is effectively a path in which we walk next to our children for a pretty long time, but by no means does that come with the guarantee of unconditional love. Even if we're connected at a Soul level, that could be for the purpose of lessons to learn in this lifetime and—hard truth, soft pillow—not necessarily the lesson of unconditional love.

The reality is that our kids do not have to love us unconditionally; ultimately, our goal is / should be to provide a really wonderful, loving, supportive guide to life for our kids—not to walk the path for them but to point out a few of the obstacles we *know* are hidden along the way and absolutely to be there supporting them through the obstacles that they alone discover.

Still with me?
Cool.

Let's talk about unconditional love in partnership and how that, too, is a myth.

The reality of a healthy, loving relationship is that it *is* so healthy and loving because of the *boundaries* in place, the boundaries that declare, "This is what feels good, supportive, and is acceptable to me."

When those boundaries are clearly defined—for yourself first—and communicated, it's very easy to feel genuinely loved and supported. And the same thing goes for your partner. When they are clear on what their own boundaries look and feel like, and can safely and comfortably communicate them, it's easy for them to feel loved and supported.

Resources like the iconic *The 5 Love Languages* by Gary Chapman as well as pretty much anything that comes out of the Gottman Institute are invaluable in discovering what kinds of things make *you* feel loved and supported and help you establish your own boundaries plus safely communicate them.

Boundaries are the scaffolding of our relationships; they are the backbone. They are the structure we need to create a level of safety and security at an emotional and neurological level. When our boundaries are violated in some way, or are otherwise disrespected and not honored, it sends a clear if unspoken message about how someone perceives us and our worth.

You prefer the phone, and the guy you swiped with insists on text.
You invoice your client, and they heckle on price or deadline.
You are committed to making healthy choices, and your partner brings home donuts.
You tell your family you need quiet time for an hour, and they knock on the door while you're in the bath.

Basic.

But what about the bigger boundaries that get crossed? The ones that feel like deal breakers, like express agreements you've made as a couple, that are not upheld? Clearly communicating your needs and having them dismissed or trivialized over and over again? Commitments (or even micro commitments) being made and repeatedly not followed through on?

This isn't "just normal relationship stuff." This is a pattern of behavior that is sending a clear message that your needs are not a priority in the relationship.

When we talk about "the work" of a relationship, we're not talking about putting up with stuff you don't like about your partner, we're talking about the relentless communication and checking in required to ensure that everyone's needs are being met and everyone's boundaries are being honored in a mutually respectful way.

And if not?

Well, *there's* the breach. *There's* the condition that didn't get met. And when the condition doesn't get met, continually and after a lot of attempts of healthy, loving communication, the love f a d e s. Fast. Because most love is, in fact, conditional.

And because we know what we know about walking our own path alongside seven billion other people walking their paths, that's usually the juncture point where those paths diverge in the woods, which is what circles us back to the "one exception" I mentioned earlier:
The one person you *can* look for, anticipate, or expect unconditional love from is the one with whom you walk the path in its entirely, come hell or high water.

Self-love and self-acceptance *is* to love yourself unconditionally.

To truly love and accept yourself is to be there—to show up when you are at your best, when you are at your worst, and everywhere in between—with loving grace and compassion, stark honesty and self-awareness, and a level of deep forgiveness born from taking personal accountability and responsibility.

Only looking for, anticipating, or expecting unconditional love from someone else—with the implicit understanding that you are not enough on your own—or that there is a void that only someone else can fill / a need that only someone else can meet is a surefire path to codependency.

What does this have to do with being alone or the feeling of belonging?

Well, if you constantly set yourself up to experience love and connection in a way that Hollywood or (barf) Instagram has taught you to experience it versus the reality of what love and connection *actually* feel like, you're setting yourself up to be disappointed. Waiting for or expecting something like this mythical unconditional love to fall from the sky keeps you separate from what is the truth, which, in turn, keeps you feeling more isolated, less connected, and far more alone.

When you can shift your gaze from an old trope you've been taught "should" be our reality toward how relationships actually work, you're reclaiming a sense of agency over your own emotional body. And when you reclaim that sense of ownership over your own emotional body, rather than react to being alone from a place of fear, lack, and scarcity, you move toward a place of love, richness, and plenty because you know that when you choose to choose you, you are choosing to love *yourself* unconditionally.

And when you choose to love yourself unconditionally, you are choosing to belong to yourself—and everyone else who comes into your life is a beautiful bonus.

Because when you belong to yourself, the truth and beauty of it is that you are never really alone.

CHAPTER NINE

JUST LIKE THE MOVIES

In my twenties, I began my foray into the working world as a Montessori teacher. The schools I taught in were in pretty ritzy areas of Toronto, and almost all of the parents of kids in our schools had ultra-cool jobs: top specialty physicians, food magazine editors, TV celebs, architects, ad agency execs, heiresses . . .

One family had a husband/wife duo of writer and director, and one of their overlapping productions was working on *Degrassi: The Next Generation*. Now, I grew up with the kids of Degrassi, and I followed them all the way through to Degrassi Junior High. When the Zit Remedy played the school dance, it was like they were playing at *my* school dance.

Spike, Wheels, Joey, Snake . . . it was a whole gang of friends I had on TV at an early age. I read all the books, watched the finale movie, can sing you the theme song right now if you want, and even bought my first house in the east end of Toronto in part by taking it as a sign that the *actual real life* Degrassi Street was only a few blocks away.

This particular parent duo knew how much I loved the show, and they knew how much I loved their little girl in my class. We had such a good working relationship, and they were/are cool AF. (I still remember the day the dad drove up in his all-black Honda minivan with tinted windows rolled down and nineties hip-hop rolling out, ready to pick up his three little girls after school and making it seem SO RAD to drive a minivan.)

So, as a thank-you gift to me at the end of the year, they invited me to a live taping of the show. I was so excited that I think I dressed up for it. On set, I realized two things:

1. Watching TV is far more exciting than *making* TV, which happens at a painfully slow pace, and
2. Nothing we see on TV is real. Like, ever.

What really drove that home—both points, actually—is that the crew had to stop every time one of the actors moved to *brush and spray her hair*. If you have ever wondered how on earth it is possible that your freshly straightened hair looks good for about five minutes before it starts to lose a little luster when a character's hair always looks so good on TV, this is why:

It takes a team of stylists to re-brush and hairspray the hot girl *lewk* every five to seven minutes.

Fast-forward a few years when my love of *The Office* was born. Once again, I've seen all the shows, watched the deleted and behind-the-scenes footage, read the books, listened to the podcasts . . . my love of this show is real, and I can quote almost every line from almost every season.

I. Love. It.

And in my deep dive fandom into what it is that makes this show so special, I have listened to the creators, writers, directors, actors, and casting directors discuss the minutia that informed each and every decision of the show's production.

Creators Ricky Gervais, Stephen Merchant, and Greg Daniels, plus some of the OG directors, talk about being intentional about having no moving walls on set. Rather, the *film crew* moves around to get natural, if awkward, shots. Did you know that most shows with a traditional set have *moveable walls* to make it easier to get flattering angles? They create a fake environment, but they make it look "real."

The casting director, Allison Jones, talks about finding unknown actors who look like normal, everyday people (versus the *Friends* model, which aimed to cast a cluster of really beautiful people). In one of her interviews, she talks about other shows she worked on, most of which wanted the super fake "beautiful people" model, and how she brought Heath Ledger to an audition and was told *he wasn't hot enough*. Heath freaking Ledger wasn't hot enough to be considered for a role in a show that was deliberately casting beautiful people.

My point?

Everything we see on TV is fake.

Yeah, yeah, I know, not a shocker. We already know *consciously* it's fake.

BUT when you revisit what we know about our *sub*conscious, we know that it soaks up information at a very early age, then cements that as truth. And we know our subconscious is always looking for proof of what we already know to be true to *be* true, thus driving home that confirmation bias.

So, if we observe something on TV, over and over again, and especially if we observe it in our formative years, chances are *even if we know what we're seeing is fake*, there is a deeper part of us that believes it to be true. And the part that believes it to be true is the part that directly influences our thoughts and subsequently our actions and behaviors.

Oh shit.

Think about everything you've learned from TV, and let's actually go back to what you very likely would have learned from TV as a kid growing up before Y2K:

How about the fact that almost every single narrative from every single Disney movie tells us women are waiting to be saved?

How about the fact that her life only *begins* once she is saved?

How about the fact that *after* her life begins, there are no challenges, just happily ever afters?

Again, I'm not saying anything new or novel here, I am simply breaking it down:

We are programmed to believe from an early age that life begins at coupledom and is smooth sailing after that partnership begins.

How about the stereotypes from *most* comedies pre-Y2K . . . and slightly beyond?

Dad is a beta bumbling idiot.

Mom is an alpha domineering bitch who has to carry the world on her shoulders with no thanks.

Fat people are funny but single.

BIPOC families behave one *specific* way, determined by their skin color or culture.

Single moms are poverty-stricken hot messes.

Single dads are heroic.

Gay men are a one-size-fits-all dramatic personality with a lisp and dramatic hands.

Gay women don't exist.

Trans people . . . wait, what?

How about the misogynistic tropes from almost every nineties' movie, and worse, before that?

It's programming.

Misrepresentative, strategic programming.

It doesn't matter if it's true, and it doesn't matter if you *think* it's true.

We are programmed to *believe* it's true and that is a legit concern because all of a sudden, when we're looking for examples of how a happy, healthy relationship (or family or friendship or work life) looks, we see nothing but perfection *or* outdated and typecast trope-y or over-the-top and unnecessarily dramatic roles of who looks like what and how that appearance/personality determines their behavior. And in its place, we are fed example after example after example of a toxic and codependent behavior pattern of enmeshment that makes us feel like *we're* doing something wrong.

Let's talk about that Venn diagram of what healthy relationships look like and reevaluate what we've been watching.

Let's look at actual divorce rates and the real-life circumstances of growing apart and start normalizing the reality that we no longer get married for the joint reasons of sharing resources and having a large family to work our farm.

Then let's start normalizing the reality of what a true dissolution of marriage looks and *feels* like and the years it takes to recover mentally, emotionally, and financially.

Then maybe, just maybe, let's stop funneling people into marriages in their twenties and pushing them toward having kids ASAP because we already know that *half* of them won't work out and *most* of those that don't work out will stop working out before age forty when the kids are young.

Then perhaps we could start normalizing what "alone" looks like and move away from it being a purgatory in between relationships, or a sad state of isolation and introversion, and be real that it's a status to celebrate all kinds of self-discovery and self-awareness and the beauty of being at peace within yourself before/while/after you're in a relationship with any other human.

You know why we'll likely *never* see that normalized on TV and in the movies?
Because it leaves very little room to sell us something.

Real life and real relationships happen within a range of emotions that, if graphed, would look like a slow or steady undulating body of water. They go up and they go down, with some degree of predictability, and they mostly stay within a particular range.

That's what peace feels like: the best kind of boring.

What sells ratings for the network and production studio, and what we are *programmed to believe is real*, is the emotional roller coaster of extreme highs and extreme lows with very little hovering around that middle mark.

That middle mark is exactly what we then interpret as "boredom" and "failure" in our own lives because we're so used to the dopamine hit and subsequent crash of peak experiences when in reality, it's the chasm between those extreme highs and lows that keeps us in a state of perpetual hunger for more, perpetual comparative lack, and perpetual FOMO.

It's the middle that allows us to feel settled without feeling like we're settling.

It's the middle that allows us to feel present without needing more than what we're experiencing.

It's the middle that allows us to get quiet enough to feel the connection to ourselves, and to something even bigger than ourselves, and makes us unwaveringly confident that we belong to ourselves.

Because when you belong to yourself, the truth and beauty of it is that you are never really alone.

CHAPTER TEN

REFRAMING MARRIAGE + PARTNERSHIP

I have a vivid memory of being in the wrapping paper aisle of the Dollar Store about a month after I called "time of death" on my first marriage and running into someone I had once considered to be a very close friend. She was someone with whom I'd shared the painful news of my divorce early on with the intention that I'd be able to lean on her through what I knew would be a difficult time.

Oh, how wrong I was.

Her reaction, when I told her, wasn't "great." It fell somewhere in the realm of her making accusations and blaming me for not trying hard enough. It was a crushing blow, completely unanticipated by me; it was pretty hurtful, disrespectful, and untrue and ultimately marked the end of that relationship. So, when I saw her there in that fateful seasonal aisle three, days before what would be my first Christmas *alone*, I wasn't "thrilled."

She offered some half-assed apology by saying, almost verbatim, "I think the reason people are so pissed at you is that you pushed the ejector button. We all had an agreement by getting married that we would suffer through this together, then cut the cake on our sixtieth wedding anniversary while looking back at all the photos on what a good life we had."

Talk about a hard truth with no soft pillow around to cushion the blow.

That comment stuck with me for years: *Is that what people think marriage is "supposed" to be?* Something to suffer through until we get to some milestone finish line, lie, and then what? Die of relief?

Let me drop a hard truth, soft pillow on you right here: if you are *suffering through* any relationship, and *particularly your marriage* . . . honey. It's time to have a serious talk about next steps.

There is so much rhetoric around the fear and judgment of being "alone." And there is so much judgment about divorce being a failure. And there is also So. Much. Judgment about what a marriage is "supposed" to be.

Let's clear this up right here, right now.

Staying trapped in a relationship that feels unsupportive, lonely, or depleting because it's what you think it's "supposed" to be is a surefire way to feel empty and hollow, and it shows your kids an unhealthy portrayal of love.

In no way is *that* a success.

Choosing to stay stuck in an unhealthy, unloving, unsupportive relationship is what creates a "broken home," not leaving a dead marriage in honor of your own boundaries and self-respect. Choosing the painful honesty of confronting what isn't working anymore and making the right decision for you, even if it isn't easy or comfortable, is the success.

The only "failure" in a marriage is the failure to honor that what marriage and partnership is "supposed" to be, which is *whatever feels mutually loving and supportive for the two people in that marriage or partnership.*

Period.

What marriage and partnership *used to* be, however, is a totally different story. Having knowledge about our brains, biology, and beliefs helps illuminate where that rhetoric and old programming comes from—the kind that tells us we're just supposed to suffer through it until we get to the sheet cake.

Imagine "back in the day" when times were hard, like really hard. We had far less access to technology that made our lives easier, we had far less access to information about our health and treatments to support it, we did far more manual labor with fewer resources, and our life-span was consequently nowhere near as long as it is today.

For timely context?

The last pandemic we had before COVID-19—the Spanish Flu in 1918—killed about fifty million people worldwide; it was so aggressive that countries were *running out of coffins* for their dead and dedicating a five-page daily spread in the newspaper for obituaries.

Fast-forward only a hundred years or so, and researchers across the world created and approved *at least three* preventative vaccine options in response to COVID-19 within a matter of *months*. That's mind-blowing progress. When technology trumps nature (for better and for worse, which really could be its own book), you know those times are a-changin'.

Anyway, back in the day when resources were few and cultivating those resources required much manual labor (and people died frequently and at a younger age), marriage was ultimately a contractual agreement for the procurement of resources. This pairing isn't a huge stretch from our pack-animal ancestors who find a suitable mate and share a life of raising the babies, keeping danger at bay, and seeking food, shelter, and comfort in between.

For humans, there are several patriarchal threads woven into our history of marriage as well; you know, back when a woman would be veiled and walked down an aisle by her father because she was literally being *given away* to her husband, the next man after her father and/or brothers she would be expected to "honor and obey."

In the 1800s, marriage was basically a ceremonial property transaction, and any money or wealth the woman *did* have going into the marriage became the *legal property of the man*. In that same vein, I'll remind you that it wasn't that long ago when "marriage" became *implied consent*, meaning once a woman was married to a man, sex became something *he was entitled to*, not something she *mutually consented to* having.

The year 1975 marked the *beginning* of recognizing the necessity of sexual consent within a marriage in the US, and it wasn't until *1993* when marital (or spousal) rape became recognized as a crime. That means until 1993—the same year that Ace of Base was topping the charts and *Mrs. Doubtfire* was selling out box offices—someone was legally entitled to have sex with their spouse *without their consent* and nobody gave a shit.

Try and think about *that* without throwing up in your mouth.

On top of *that*, different religious and cultural expectations throughout time and history exacerbated this entitled "property ownership" model by expressly forbidding divorce, often under the guise of social shunning or damnation, effectively trapping women in marriages that were oppressive, highly dysfunctional, or worse.[3]

I dare you to look up "coverture" and go down the rabbit hole of the legal understanding, embedded into the fabric of colonial society, that women did not legally exist for *years*, which had all kinds of ramifications

....
3 And if you think this—the social shunning of a woman in modern society post-divorce— doesn't exist in our current society, you are living in a fantasy land. Whether you were left or you did the leaving, there are still *several* embedded cultural narratives that somehow, in either case, claim it was your fault as a woman for the marriage not working.

on human/family/sexual rights and property ownership. The mere fact that abortion is *still* a subject of contentious discussion around so many dinner tables and political pulpits, without ever the mention of male sterilization, is a testament to *how long* it takes to undo "what was" from our cultural and social beliefs and norms.

Think about what that does to both the female *and* male psyche.
For generations.
Ugh. Ick.

It isn't rocket science. There are deep patriarchal roots entrenched in *most* Western cultural traditions to the point that we don't even realize why we're doing them because it's just the way we've always done them. *All the Single Ladies* by *New York Times* best-selling author Rebecca Traister is an excellent place for a deep dive into the roots of marriage and its various implications throughout North America.

Over time, marriage evolved into partnership, and as the rights of women increased, options expanded from being a mother tending the home and raising children to being just about *anything*, inside or outside the home. Or both.

Like it or not, having money is usually equal to having freedom, power, agency, and the ability to say yes or no out of *desire*, not necessity. When women were able to make, and *keep*, their own money, and technology accelerated at an exponential rate, and social justice started to become a topic of conversation, and same-sex marriages started to be recognized, and men were able to get paternity leave, and, and, and . . .

. . . that resource sharing became far less important, we started to create a brand-new model of how humans live and subsequently, a brand-new model of procuring our *own* resources.

Remember learning about Maslow's Hierarchy of Needs in your first-year psych class?

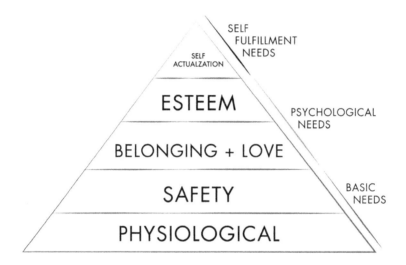

Maslow proposed that our needs are tiered and that we meet them in the order of what is most important to our physical and eventually emotional/mental/spiritual survival, starting with basic physiological and safety needs (food, water, warmth, rest, shelter, security), then moving through psychological needs (belonging, love, connection, feeling of accomplishment), then all the way up to self-fulfillment needs and self-actualizing through spirituality, creativity, expressing and "achieving" one's fullest potential.

Guess what, folks? As our world, culture, society, and lives have evolved (on average) over time, we've progressed through meeting those basic physiological needs and tend to dwell more in meeting our psychological and self-actualization needs.

Therefore, since you're reading this book, congratulations on being at a point in your life in which *you have the luxury of having an existential crisis*. I'm being very sincere here—it's actually a moment of celebration that you've come so far in your life that you have, and I'll say it again, *the luxury* of having an existential crisis and *are able to* question your role or belonging in this world because it means you are operating from a place in which your needs for physical survival are attended to and met, which is a luxury too many of us take for granted.

Keep in mind also that "back in the day," when marriage was *forever*, "forever" meant living to about age forty or fifty tops, and most of that time was spent laboring to meet basic needs for human survival, relying on a solid division of labor to do so, and included surviving massive historical events like world wars and the Great Depression.

"Forever" means something *so* different now.

On average, women tend to marry around age twenty-six and men at twenty-nine; our life spans are predicted to be seventy-eight to eighty-two, again, on average. Committing to someone at age twenty-six until death literally *does you part* a half a century later, with a lot more financial independence, freedom, resources, ease, and options in between already starts to change the game.

So.

What do we know right now that will help us reframe marriage and partnership, and the endings thereof, which ultimately allows us to reframe being alone and the truth and beauty of belonging?

We know that:

- We are biologically programmed for connection and procreating, steering us *genetically* toward wanting to partner.
- We are social beings evolving from social groups and that at a deep genetic level, we equate "belonging" with survival.
- We've been culturally conditioned to see "marriage" as belonging, aka survival.
- Our human software (physical and tangible stuff) evolves quickly.
- Our human *hardware* (emotional and intangible stuff) evolves at a glacially slow rate.
- Our brain loves status quo because status quo feels easy and easy feels good.
- To preserve the status quo, our brains keep us in behavior pattern loops to do things the way we've always done them.
- Our subconscious constantly looks for confirmation bias, finding examples of what we already believe to be true to *be* true.
- Our subconscious alerts us to something against status quo and triggers a physiological fear response.
- Mainstream and social media perpetuates old cultural "norms" in a completely fake way and is designed to capitalize on and profit from each of our fears.
- We always have agency and control of *how we respond to anything and everything.*

That's what we're working with.

No matter what you believe consciously, i.e., "being single is awesome, being alone feels good, ending a not-great long-term relationship makes sense," if those beliefs are only held at the *conscious* thought level but conflict with a more deeply held *subconscious* belief that is entirely likely being carried over from generations past when being alone literally did mean rejection or death, it doesn't matter what you *think*. You are still going to experience emotional pain, turmoil, and likely anxiety about being alone (in the context of singlehood) unless your subconscious beliefs are fully aligned and have evolved into healing, accepting, and embodying that *being single is safe.*

It is a huge deal.

If you don't feel neurologically or emotionally safe, you cannot fully embody a new thought or pattern of behavior because your internal safety systems will not let you.

Cue a level of self-compassion and forgiveness for any feelings or judgments of those feelings, then appreciate that you come by them honestly, if not *genetically*.

For real.

Starting with that overall context of where we're coming from (with respect to how our brains work and what we're culturally/biologically programmed to believe), where we are now (grace and self-compassion), and where we're going (ready for a new thought pattern and a new way of *be*ing), here are three questions to ask that make it surprisingly easy to unlearn what we *knew* to be true about marriage and partnership and start to reframe what we *want to be true* about marriage and partnership.

REFRAME NUMBER ONE: WHAT IF ONE "FOREVER" RELATIONSHIP ISN'T WHAT WE NEED?

A number of years ago, I heard renowned psychotherapist Esther Perel suggest something that would change my outlook on marriage and partnership: She introduced the notion that most of us need *three* partners over the course of our adult lives, and if we're *lucky*, we find all three in the same person.

Marriage and divorce stats tell us that finding a partner is fairly easy but that staying with that same partner forever is not. Hence, the near 50 percent divorce rate for first marriages and *60 percent* for second marriages.

Hard truth, soft pillow: *Very few people will meet the one person early on with whom they can grow at the same, or supportive rate, as one another.* The rest of us will find a partner, outgrow them (or be outgrown), and move on to the next.

Ooooooofffff . . . but also?
F r e e d o m. Freedom from the chain of largely unrealistic and antiquated expectations called "forever."

We grow and evolve *so much* in our lives. We (particularly women) are in a near constant state of flux in healing from our past and growing toward our future, informed by the circumstances and our ability to integrate it all in the present. Are you the same person you were five years ago? Five months ago? Five weeks ago?

Can you even imagine who you'll be five years from *now*? In ten?

When you are living a purpose-driven and meaningful life, you grow quickly, which also means you *die a lot of deaths* along the way because there cannot be rebirth without death on the long walk home to your*self*.

Knowing that that is the reality of how we *become* ourselves, especially if you identify as a woman, I bet you also know the many layers of mixed emotions that go alongside that death and rebirth process. If you want to get hella granular with this concept, keep in mind that once a month, as a woman, you *shed a literal layer* of yourself. Before the days of hormones in food and unnatural lighting in indoor environments, women's menstrual cycles were fairly predictable in their alignment with the lunar calendar, and the full moon was a time of massive release on a physical and emotional level.

We are constantly letting go of what was, and we are preparing ourselves to receive what is or what will be. And in that process, that wild and alchemical process of creating ourselves as we go, we need a partner who can grow at the same rate—or who is able to support that growth and for whom we can support theirs—in a mutually aligned timeline.

Uh, I hate to be the bearer of obvious news here, but the near 50 percent divorce rate would indicate that that doesn't happen *most* of the time. Most of us meet someone, learn a lot of lessons and, much like the little hermit crab, outgrow the shell of that relationship and move on.

Our old historical, sociocultural, patriarchal, religious, misogyny-centric stories tell us that leaving that relationship is some indication of failure, but *literally every other marker* of success, emotional and mental health, and morality tells us otherwise: that to stay in a relationship in which we feel like we can neither support nor be supported or otherwise feel trapped would be the wrong thing to do.

When we live by the old rules and feel the weight of the pressure that funnels us into marriages in our twenties (before we're even fully formed adults), then feel the weight of the pressure that tells us now is the right time to have kids, then feel the weight of the pressure that tells us divorce is a sign of a broken home or failure, *that is what sets us up for failure* over and over again.

Again, it's staying stuck in a dead-end marriage—not leaving it—that creates a broken home.

Each of us deserves to be *loved* by someone.
Each of us deserves to be loved by someone who is the *best* at loving us.
If there's someone who can love us better than the one we're with, *that* is the person we deserve to be loved by.

Knowing before we even begin that the reality is that we will require different kinds of relational support as we grow and evolve, plus *knowing* that (currently) about 50 percent of first marriages *end*, it is about fucking time we change the bloody narrative by changing our expectations.

What if we entered into marriage as a sacred and loving union framed with vows that sought to honor our love and support one another for *as long as it makes sense . . .* or something a little more eloquent than that?

What if we were to have open and frank conversations with our partner about what specifically they needed to feel supported as part of a regular check-in on the emotional health and well-being of our relationship? What if that involved speaking to a third party like a therapist/coach/pastor/mentor on a regular basis *before* crisis mode hit as part of an ongoing gift to the health of our relationship?

What if, and this is the big one, we shifted our focus from *finding* the one to *being* the one?

Think on that.

What if our primary relationship was with our Self . . . and anyone else became the vanilla buttercream icing with rainbow sprinkles on our already-delicious *cake?*

While I was studying for my master's certification in my neuro-linguistic programming training, a classmate described how she'd met her partner late in life, had a son later in life, and had felt *so much shame in delaying those milestones.*

And there I was, juxtaposed against her story by becoming married relatively young in life, having my kids relatively young in life, and then becoming divorced by thirty-four, and I felt *so much shame in rushing those milestones.*

That's when an epiphany hit me like a tsunami of peace and clarity: *What if* one of the three *partners we require in the holistic growth and development of our adult self is* our own self?

What if there is an actual season of adulthood *designed* to be spent alone, all with the intention of becoming an expert in ourselves in the most intimate way, so that we can fully appreciate what it is *we need* to feel loved and then share that with a future partner in addition to how we can specifically best love another?

What if we focused on "the one" being *the one* that looks back at us in the mirror, then enter into partnership with someone else with the understanding that we are simply two independent people choosing to live and love an interdependent life?

Knowing the adage that "wherever you go, there you are" and that the only person guaranteed, *guaranteed* to be there from the moment you're born until the moment you die is yourself, it suddenly seems like a no-brainer that the most significant relationship in your life is the one you have with yourself, and it is worthy of your time, commitment, and love.

REFRAME NUMBER TWO: WHAT IF YOU CAN HAVE IT ALL, JUST NOT AT THE SAME TIME?

A friend of mine has dual American/Canadian citizenship, and we share a love of Americans, America, and how "extra" it is—you feel it as soon as you cross the border into the US. We often joke about how much *more* there is in the US and how even grocery shopping in the US is extra. For example, the yogurt aisle in a Canadian grocery store is "here's a shelf or two that offer a few kinds of yogurt," while in the States, it's a literal wall of yogurt options.

With so many options, how do you know what to choose?

The glitch in the feminist movement is that, here in the fourth wave thereof, it has opened so many options . . . *without fully changing any of the old expectations* because those old expectations take a very long time to change.

There's an even more intensely felt pressure to perform because now that you can do anything, you're expected to do *everything*, and it's an impossible dream to fulfill while adhering to the already-ingrained sociocultural expectations that you go to school, get a good job, meet your person, raise awesome kids, buy a great house in the right neighborhood, travel the world, have a thriving online presence, make time for self-care, have regular, mind-blowing sex, hit those $10K+ months, rescue a dog and run its Instagram account, eat clean, work out daily, etc.

Many of us feel caught in the chasm of having too many expectations and trying to do them all at once.

With so many options, how do you know what to choose?

I will never forget the day my first shipment of my first book arrived via delivery to my house. A man named Ken knocked on my door to tell me he had a large collection of boxes in the trunk. I was so excited that I didn't even put on my shoes; I ran outside with him, cut open one of the boxes (still in the trunk of his little blue hatchback), and held the first copy of my first book with its creamy, heavyweight paper as the crown achievement of my professional life.

I started bawling. It was such an intense emotional release of the thirty-five years of lived experience that had gone into that book, and now there it was, ready to launch into the world. Ken very tenderly said to me, "Take your time; enjoy this moment."

Then we got talking about his own life. He told me that he'd grown up in India and had moved to Canada when he was seventeen. He told me that growing up, life had been so clear: He'd been expected to become a lawyer, doctor, or engineer. And when he moved here to North America, those expectations expanded from what had been so linearly defined into "here, you can be *anything*."

Very stoically he said, "I don't know which was harder: feeling forced into being *one* thing or feeling forced into *being whatever I want*." It was a beautiful, intimate moment shared between strangers.

With so many options, how do you know what to choose?

Sometimes our options create freedom and sometimes our options create their own brand of oppression.

Another one of those viral internet memes I've happened upon that doesn't seem to have an author is "We expect women to work like they don't have children and raise children as if they don't work."

Oof, there it is.

When we open the floodgates of options and choices, it's a really, really *good* thing, and it's also an incredibly slow-going process for our brains and cultural expectations to play catch-up. And so, we get stuck, for a few different generations, in this liminal space of needing to have it all.

Like, now.

And being the resourceful, resilient, highly adaptable species we are, we somehow figure it out.
We find a way to have the job, have the family, have the care of self . . . and sidebar?

Along comes the pandemic and just about annihilates the women who've been doing it all. Closing small businesses or demanding next-level pivots in the scope and service and how they reach their client base largely affected female-owned and operated businesses *while* these women raised kids at home, monitored online learning, and for many, cared for aging parents and relatives at the same time. Again, cue the secondary pandemic of the mental and emotional health crises that we've yet to unravel.

All that to say, the pressure you're feeling is real. It's an overwhelming amount of nearly impossible expectations to meet and live up to.

With all those options and knowing everything you now know about the brain and everything you now know about the glacially slow pace at which we play catch-up, neurologically, to our evolving culture, what if you could consciously tune out the expectations of others around you and establish your own metrics of what success not only looks like but *feels* like?

What if you got hella clear on what success feels like for you, specifically, then intentionally lived your life not checking off boxes on the ladder-style list of what comes next, but instead chose—out of all the options available to you—to do what feels really fucking good, and you do so on a timeline that works for you, specifically, while being consciously aware that you are being divinely guided and protected the whole damn time.

Note: If you're someone without kids, or even someone without the desire to have kids, no problem. Adjusting your expectations and being comfortable with the life *you desire* and choose to live, because of how it aligns with your unique values and how it feels *for you specifically*, is enough, regardless of any opinion anyone may feel entitled to share with you.

Everything we do requires energy (and energy usually means time, attention, and money):
Having a career.

Discovering yourself.
Being a partner.
Attending to your living space.
Seeing the world.
Investing in your future.
Having pets.
Raising kids.
Caring for loved ones.
Posting on social media.
Maintaining friendships.
Building generational wealth.
Living healthy lives.

It all requires energy.

And we each have a finite amount of energy to invest in each of these areas. Giving and giving and giving is a surefire route to burnout and is very often a red flag alerting you to some codependent patterns that may be driving the bus in the back of your subconscious.

Getting crystal fucking clear on how you want your life to feel—and doing the inner work that makes this a safe reality for you subconsciously—is what allows you to embody the truest version of yourself as well as that vision you just can't stop dreaming about, no matter how simple or complex it may be.

Once you know what your unique vision looks or feels like, you can establish the loving, healthy boundaries required to *protect* your energy and solidify the very real truth that you *can* have it all (just not at the same time), which clearly isn't a failure, it's literally just a consequence of modern life.

REFRAME NUMBER THREE: WHAT IF THERE'S NO SUCH THING AS "THE ONE?"

Walk through this thought exercise with me:

There are about seven billion people in the world.

Let's say half of those people are a gender you're attracted to, so 3.5 billion.

Now, let's narrow our scope to people in the same age/resource/language category (i.e., people with whom statistics show you're more likely to partner), and we're probably whittling that number down to one million, worst-case scenario.

Out of that million people who check the right boxes on paper, let's narrow it down again to geographical location, even though we know we (usually) live in a highly migratory world in which it's not unlikely to meet anyone from anywhere, and we'll narrow our scope once again to 500 thousand.

Of those 500 thousand people, let's adjust for qualities that really draw us and our attraction toward someone, and we're at (again, worst case) 10,000 people.

Without exaggerating, it's entirely conceivable that *there are easily 10,000 people* with whom you could enter into a loving, healthy partnership.

If that feels too daunting, zoom in even more radically and adjust for factors like living in a small town, epigenetics, genealogy, family history, socioeconomic status, qualities specific to you like "doesn't have kids but wants them" or "must play guitar." Even with those sweeping measures in place, it's not only possible but probable that *there are easily a hundred people* who would make the ideal partner for you.

So, is it also possible, and even probable, especially knowing what we know about our own individuation and evolution and need for different partners at different times, that there is literally no such thing as "the one?"

Is it possible and even probable that the concept of "the one" is yet another storyline force-fed to us as a carry-over from old standards and definitions of marriage, played like the heartstrings of a violin by the business of Hollywood, and that maybe, just maybe, "the one"—gasp!— isn't a real thing?

Maybe, just maybe, is it possible and even probable that there can be less pressure to meet the one perfect person when you shift your attention to the fact that there are easily 100 people who meet your definition of a partner?

And if we zoom out even further from the statistics and specifics and back to an understanding of the soul contract or agreement we made coming into this life, is it possible and even probable that a part of this grand plan is to connect or reconnect you to a series of special and formative relationships *throughout your life*, thus further freeing you from the shackles of performatively finding the one and only person for you?

Is it possible and even probable that when we follow the cosmic bread-crumbs of our life and listen to those little heart whispers or voices that seem to come from nowhere and everywhere at the same time—that intuitive *knowing*—that we're walking the exact path at the exact time and being divinely guided and supported all along?

It doesn't mean it doesn't feel unfair, uncomfortable, or downright scary in the meantime. Tell me, what so far about your human experience *hasn't* had some degree of unfairness, discomfort, or fear so far?

The point is, what if we consciously choose to see the forest through our own trees, consciously choose to surrender, and consciously choose to trust that our life is working out exactly as it's supposed to and that this notion of meeting "the one" that is being shoved down our throat by, oh say, a multibillion-dollar wedding and algorithm-based dating industry is mayyyyybe not without its own self-serving agenda?

The reality is that *we have many soul mates*; a soul mate is a person we're connected to at a soul level for a reason, a season, or a lesson. We're tied to them, often from a previous life experience, in a way that doesn't necessarily involve romance or intimacy. You know those people who become your greatest teachers through all the challenges they bring into your life?

Soul mate: there to be a vehicle for your own growth and expansion, even when that growth and expansion, frankly, sucks.

When we shift into appreciating the *quality* of the relationship versus the quantity (for example, the length) of the relationship, we can also shift into garnering that we get exactly what we need from each relationship, for better or worse, that is specifically designed to bring us home to ourselves.

We have the *luxury* of marrying for love, not for the safety and security of sharing resources.

We have the *luxury* of choosing to do it differently than our ancestors.

We have the *luxury* of taking our time and making decisions that are based in the desire of what *we want*, not what our history or cultural narrative tells us that we want.

That means you have the privilege and the luxury to start normalizing the process of learning to be in true partnership with yourself: know yourself, love yourself, enjoy spending time with yourself, and cultivate the feeling of belonging to *you*.

Because when you belong to yourself, the truth and beauty of it is that you are never really alone.

CHAPTER ELEVEN

HOW TO END SINGLE SHAMING

Growing up, my best friend and I spent as much time as possible together. Our parents were friends and liked to go away during March Break together, and since both of our families were so close, we spent most of our school-year weekends simply going back and forth to one another's houses. Those were the days of being able to ride your bike through the neighborhood, playing capture the flag with a bunch of kids on the block, and being signaled to come home only when the streetlights came on.

God bless that old school eighties' childhood.

One day my friend somehow left her bike at my place, so the next day I returned it by hopping on my bike and navigating her empty bike beside me by the handlebars. It was only a few blocks away through some pretty quiet streets on the route I deliberately took, which made it feel a little extra creepy when a much older man slowed down behind me in his car, then pulled up beside me.

I don't remember his wording exactly, but I do remember his accusatory tone, demanding to know why I had two bikes, where the second one came from, and where I was going. Why he felt entitled to any of this information is beyond me; he clearly judged and interpreted me having two bikes as me *stealing* a bike.

I was in the primo people-pleasing years of my life and had a near-crippling fear of authority/adults, so despite my very pure intentions of returning my best friend's bicycle, I felt threatened by his presence and felt compelled to tell him *all the details* of how this purple Norco came to be in my possession, where I'd come from, and where I was going.

Eventually, he left me alone and drove away, and when I got home, after dropping off the extra bike, I told my dad what had happened, and he very clearly, very calmly looked me right in my eyes and said, "You don't owe anyone an explanation for anything," which through my adult lens I now know was his polite way of telling me the more appropriate response for that creepy old guy would have been "it's none of your fucking business."

There are always going to be people in your life who feel entitled to having more of you, having more access *to* you, or enmeshing themselves more closely in your life without your express permission. You know who those people are because they are the ones who can't seem to take a hint, the ones who tell you what your ex is up to on social media long after you've broken up, the ones who want to know when you're going to try again after a miscarriage. They are the ones who ask for a list of where you buy your furniture and art when you post something on Instagram, who are cool to read the book that you bought after you read it, who order back-to-back drinks at dinner then want to split the bill evenly, or who want to "pick your brain" about your area of expertise without paying you for your time. They are the same ones who think they know you and feel entitled to judge the decisions you make about *your* life.

Some people, a lot of people actually, have no idea where the line is, and so they keep crossing it over and over until you show them where it is and tell them to stop.

Those lines are called boundaries.

Hard truth, soft pillow? *People treat us the way we allow them to treat us.*

If you feel like your personal life, intimate information, and/or any other details you hold close are consistently under attack or even up for discussion and debate, that would be a sign that boundaries need a little love and attention from you.

I get asked, both as a single woman and emotional health advocate, about single shaming a lot. And even though it comes up so much, it always takes me by surprise because even after having been single for what feels like an eternity, I don't feel like I ever experience *overt* single shaming.

If we're talking about *covert* single shaming, the kind that is less spoken about and is rather more embedded into the fabric of our lives versus the threads of conversation, then yes, *that* is alive and well.

The difference?

Covert (think *hidden*) single shaming is present in things like restaurants offering all their takeout specials for two, not getting invited to dinner parties because you don't have a partner, only being included in social gatherings when it's "girls' night," or feeling used by your married/partnered friends who act like they need an escape from their married life and almost latch on to you to provide or perform the experience of what "single" looks like for them.

This kind of single shaming is harder to spot because it *is* so embedded into the fabric of our social lives. I mean, how many people are calling you up to say, "Hey, I'm having a dinner party, and I'd love to invite you, but I think it'll be weird for you to come solo, so I'm going to invite another couple instead." Your phone kinda just. stops. ringing.

As a sidebar, why does this happen? Why do couples often feel like they can't include non-couples in their life, and the single woman in particular? Is it rooted in feeling threatened by the presence of a single woman? Are they afraid she's going to have a cathartic emotional release being around other couples? Are they afraid she's going to seduce one of the husbands in between the appetizer and the entrée? If the presence of an unattached woman feels like a threat to your relationship, for either of you, it's time to have a good hard look at the foundation of your relationship to see where the cracks are.

And further, why is it deemed acceptable to hang out with this unmarried woman only on a girls' night? When you're a single woman, literally *every* night is girls' night; it feels like thinly veiled escapism when your married friends are suddenly no longer available to hang out with you unless their husbands are gone for the night or sequestered to the basement while you have "girl time" in the living room. And nine times out of ten? "Girl time" quickly morphs into "married girl complaining about her marriage to single girl time."

How about when you go away for a "girls'" trip and a couple of the married ones don't make it back to your Airbnb that night because they're *hooking up with* other people and sleeping at their places instead. It is a real thing that happens, and when you're the single one in the group, it feels like you're Patrick Fugit's character in *Almost Famous* in that you are being used as an excuse for Penny Lane, and your girlfriends, to get away from their lives.

Spoiler:
None of this feels good for the single one, and *all of this* is a conversation about boundaries:
- *This* feels safe and good for me,
- *that* does not.

- *This* behavior is acceptable,
- *that* behavior is not.

In recent years we have opened up a macro-level conversation on consent. While consent has become top of mind in our cultural lexicon over the past few years (did we even have a word or context for consent in the eighties and nineties?), and while it started through the context of sexual interactions, it has extended into so many other areas of our lives, which is a very good thing.

This is a part of *that* because what we're really talking about in the overall context of consent is communicating and honoring individual boundaries.

So, whereas *covert* single shaming is basically silent exclusion from regular adult social life, *overt* single shaming is directly proportionate to the boundaries that you alone are responsible for setting.

It often seems that the conversation around overt single shaming is focused on "why would someone say/do this to me?" But really? The missing piece of that conversation is "why did I *allow* someone to say/do that to me, and what would I do differently the next time?"

Literally, the *only* thing we have full control or agency over in our lives is how we choose to react and respond. In every area of our lives. That's it. You can't control what people say, how they act, or what they believe, you can only control how you specifically react.

If you notice that there are more than a few conversations happening with people prying into your life by questioning your relationship status or wondering how someone like you has been single for so long . . .

. . . you need to set some boundaries.

Trust me, I understand that when these conversations come up, it can feel like someone picking at the scab of your emotional wound. It doesn't feel good, and it often feels quite hurtful.

"You're so beautiful and accomplished; why are *you* still single?"

Most people aren't asking these probing questions or making what feels like callous statements with the intention of hurting you. Most people actually intend it to be a compliment as in "I see how amazing you are; how is it possible that someone equally as wonderful hasn't scooped you up yet?"

What they don't know is that even those well-intentioned comments can feel like opening the likely wounded and self-shaming dialogue of *"what the fuck is wrong with me that despite my beauty, success, and general awesomeness, someone hasn't scooped me up yet? What the hell else do I have to DO to prove I am actually enough?"*

Most people just have no idea what feels appropriate for *you*.
So, let me ask: Do *you* know what feels appropriate for you?

Boundaries start right there: with what feels good for you. What honors, protects, and respects your *unique* sense of what feels right and good for you?

When someone is openly:
- questioning (Why are you still single?)
- judging (You seem picky; your standards might be a little too high.)

- suggesting (Well, have you ever tried online dating?)
- advising (I think you need to be more open to meeting someone.)
- shaming (You're not getting any younger; maybe it's time to get serious and compromise a little.)

. . . then it is your responsibility to yourself to communicate what is or isn't acceptable to you.

I told you that I don't experience overt single shaming because my personal boundaries in this department are *so damn good*. (I also told you that my own personal boundaries with respect to more covert single shaming needed some work. See? We're all just figuring it out as we go, living and learning.)

I know very well, after *a lot* of inner work and with the support of my very loving family and my very loving friend and author of *Single is the New Black: Don't Wear White 'til it's Right*, Dr. Karin Anderson Abrell, that the reason I (and very likely you) am/are still single (even if we desire partnership) is because we *just haven't met the right person yet.*

Period.

That truth is *so secure* for me—that the only reason I am single is because I just haven't met the right person yet—that even if someone

- *questions* why I am single? I actually *do* take it as a compliment. As in "hell, yeah, I know I'm awesome; can you imagine how awesome Mr. Right must be to make it an equal match?"

- *judges* my standards? Yeah, no. I didn't come this far only to get this far, thanks. You obviously know nothing about me personally, meaning I don't need to take what *you* say personally.
- *suggests* I try something different? See above. If your opinion matters to me, it's because you *know* me, and if you *know* me, you already know I am leave-no-stone-unturned-level thorough, exhaustively.
- *advises or shames?* "Well isn't *that* interesting . . . " We are all reflections of one another like little mirrors, and if someone is shaming or advising your relationship status or goals in an unsolicited manner, it offers keen insights as to what they are experiencing. I instantly have compassion for what they must be feeling in their own life that makes them feel like it's acceptable to advise or shame me in mine.

Relationships are one of the only areas of life in which effort does not beget success, and no matter what anyone offers up to you to say otherwise, relationships are not algorithmic because humans are not algorithmic. It's an uncomfortable and sometimes ugly truth, but it is a truth nonetheless: *In relationships, effort does not beget success, and action does not beget results.*

Contrary to what too many dating coaches (not all, but a lot) try to sell you, you can't *do* more to *get* more success in relationships; it's a very masculine energy dynamic that *usually* works in other areas of life:
- If I *do more* marketing, I *get more* sales.
- If I *do more* studying, I *get more* desired grades.

Do/achieve, do/achieve, do/achieve. Repeat.

But love doesn't work like that; trust me, I've tried.

Nobody else around you may relate to or understand that, and *it doesn't matter*. Your boundaries are based on what feels good for you, specifically. And if you can wrap your head around the fact that you can't "do more" to get more, that there's no algorithm, then that's going to help establish what feels good for you while you're setting those unique boundaries.

Knowing what you know now about The Plan, The Path, and the very nature of the unfolding of our lives, there's nothing you can *do more of* in order to illicit a particular outcome. You just have to *be*.

It's. So. Frustrating. I know. And it's often downright painful. Ugh.

That is why you're reading this book, or at least why I'm writing this book: to offer solace in what it looks like to *be*, and what it looks like, reimagined, to *be* alone. Clearly communicated boundaries that are a loving, healthy reflection of who you are and what you value are a significant part of cultivating the relationship you have with yourself.

And while (frustratingly) there is no algorithm that says, "Okay, cool, *if* you have a loving relationship with yourself, *then* you can have a relationship with someone else," it does cultivate a deep and profound sense of inner peace in knowing that you love, accept, and belong to yourself.

And when you belong to yourself, the truth and beauty of it is that you are never really alone.

CHAPTER TWELVE

ALONE PHYSICALLY

You know those pivotal "where were you when . . . " moments in history we all share?

It's safe to say the 2020 US election was one of those moments. Remember how *insane* that was? The months leading up to the election, the months just following, and the night itself were Just. So. Memorable.

And I remember very well where I was the night/morning after the 2020 US election:

 . . . I was sexting with Jason.

Oh yeah, baby; I was in the throes of an intensely sexual conversation with Jason, a guy from New York City I'd met online a few months earlier.

Now, Jason wasn't *just* a guy from New York City. Jason was an athletic, 6'4", broad-shouldered, unmarried, and childless forty-two-year-old finance guy from New York City with a lowwwww baritone voice and chocolate-brown eyes who defended old ladies from rude teens at the drug store, surfed, loved football, openly told me *how much he wanted an instant family* and to be the kind of loving stepdad he'd grown up with, and who casually split his time between Manhattan, *the Hamptons*, and his *fucking cabin upstate*.

That is my own personal brand of relational kryptonite.

Jason was the *exact* physical manifestation of my ideal man, right down to the length of his . . . well, let's just say I was made *keenly* aware of Jason's proportions, and trust me when I say, "Life was coming up Leisse."

We had "super liked" each other on Tinder—super liked *each other*, do you know how rare that is?—in July, and we had talked about the possibility / definite impossibility of meeting IRL because it was mid-pandemic and crossing the border meant a two-week quarantine to shelter in one place. And while I am a hopeful romantic, I'm also not an idiot; inviting a stranger from the internet to come and live with me for two weeks doesn't fall under the umbrella of "quirky first dates" that I am otherwise open to having.

As tends to happen with meeting online, the conversation kind of fizzled out after a few text exchanges. But we didn't unmatch, plus we had swapped phone numbers, so come the day of the US election, Little Miss Recovering Codependent over here sends a text his way saying,

"Just checking in" to let a certain tall sexy guy know she's thinking of him during this truly historic event. And he wrote back. So, I wrote back. And then so did he.

And eventually, there we were, watching this historical shit show unfold late into the evening, and what were we supposed to do, not flirt?

Yeah, no.
It *obviously* got flirty, then subsequently *flirtier* the later and darker it got.

And then the photos started heading my way: the photos that proved just how, ahem, "proportionate" things were for my American friend who was standing in his bathroom between the mirror and the epic soaker tub and walk-in glass shower and telling me all of the things he was going to do to me while we were in that *money* shower/tub combination.

Meow.

Now, I know that it *should have been* a sign that these photos (and eventually, video) were shot with him in the nude, wearing nothing but his *white Crocs.*

But in my defense, this was around the time when Questlove had been photographed in Crocs on some red carpet *and* after Jason and I had had the conversation about his propensity toward great and bougie taste in Reigning Champ cashmere track suits (with nothing underneath, OMG), so I honestly thought *maybe* it was a NYC fashion-forward thing that hadn't yet migrated up north.

And then it got real.

Not only was Jason a great photographer (blush), but he was also, uh, an *incredibly* gifted and descriptive writer. I don't want to brag or anything BUT man, I can *throw down* in sexting, and this guy not only met me where I was but was able to take it even further.

So, it was *on*.
And it was *hot*.
And it was *fun*.

And I hadn't been laid in so long. It just felt right.

Naturally, hanging on to the death rattle of my own toxic relational patterns of codependency in intimate partnerships, I thought our exchanges were the beginning of a real thing. Current me looks back on past me with tender compassion, knowing now that it was very likely this sexy online tryst with Jason that *enabled me* to break said patterns, but nonetheless, at the time, I was misguidedly thinking, "I did it. I met *the* guy."

Whoops.

You may not be shocked to learn that after I deliciously gave it up via text to Mr. Cabin Upstate that night (and again in the morning while he was on a Zoom call—hey-ohhhhh), I didn't really hear from him again. I had communicated that all of that had happened a little faster than I would've liked and that I'd love to talk on the phone for some reassurance. And while he said he'd call, he never did.

And that was that.

With that abrupt end to what I had 100 percent embellished and roman-ticized in my head to being the beginning of a real-ationship, which, in fairness, was fueled not only by his physicality but by the express desire he communicated in *wanting to be* an amazing stepdad, I was *pissed*.

Having received that kind of male (cough, sexual) attention in among *all* of the qualities I specially envision my partner to embody, I felt like I'd had a glimpse of, then was robbed of, an experience that I just couldn't give to myself.

Because when you are physically alone, no matter how confident, secure, or empowered you are in your alone-ness—hard truth, soft pillow? *You can't clap with one hand.*

There are some things you just can't do for yourself.

I had one of my real-deal talks with myself. There was a serious letdown after this electronic hookup, exacerbated by the never-ending pandemic and the painful reality that I would be physically alone for who knows how long. I kicked into "how do I use Emotional Alchemy here? How is it that I *want* to feel, and how do I *create that feeling* in the absence of an actual man?"

The feeling I wanted, frankly, was the weight of a man to cuddle up with, so how did I create it? I Amazon Primed myself a six-foot U-shaped body pillow, weighted blanket, and a bottle of cologne I'd go gaga to smell on a real-life six-foot-four man. I became that little monkey in the lab who, deprived of his real mother, snuggles up to the sock monkey version the researcher left in her place.

And you know what?
It worked.

I spritzed the cologne on the body pillow, named it my "boyfriend pillow," cuddled up with it around me on the couch or in my bed, and cozied up underneath the weighted blanket. I basically recreated the sensory feeling my body *required* to feel grounded, whole, and secure, then backed that up with breath work and meditations for my root chakra to heal and anchor that feeling of internal safety and security.

As I say, sometimes there is a threshold for even the most confident and self-assured among us when we are physically alone, and there's no shame in feeling the discomfort of that threshold. It doesn't make you less than or not enough or needy or weird; it makes you *human.*

When we are, for one reason or another, separated physically by geography, timing, or fucking pandemics (because hard truth, soft pillow? You *know* COVID-19 isn't the last one we'll see in our lifetime), *the feeling of physical isolation is profoundly real.* Feeling the weight and warmth of a human body on your human body is one of *the* simplest and greatest pleasures of all time.

The absence of human touch is detrimental to our own body chemistry and physiology, let alone our emotional health and well-being.

And it's not just the absence of human touch we feel in these times of physical isolation; it's the absence of *intimacy* we feel. Even if you get really good at making time to cultivate a relationship with yourself, and you consciously have a self-pleasure practice that feels amazing, there is a degree of intimacy that feels like it can only be created in the company of another, which is a painful reality:

There are times in life when it *just feels better* to be with someone.

As a single parent, I have to have difficult conversations on my own in blended-family life and in healing my own complex family trauma, and there are events that feel like they deserve or are entitled to be shared and not spent on my own. The ensuing feelings of how unfair that is can really weigh on a person, so having an action plan or go-to strategy can help immensely as you learn to create emotional intimacy with yourself, even in the physical or emotional absence of someone else.

How does it look to create emotional intimacy with yourself in the physical or emotional absence of someone else?

Start by imagining *what you want it to feel like*. In the example of having to make a difficult phone call, what I personally want is to feel safe. Protected. Secure. Unfuckwithable. Cared for. Like I have someone who has my back, someone who makes me feel like I don't have to take it so seriously.

Then ask what *would* make you feel like those feelings were present? For me, invariably the answer is "having my partner here *with* me while I make the phone call." So, I imagine who that partner would be, what he would be like, and how, specifically, he would create an environment in which we could make light of the situation while, at the same time, I felt safe, protected, secure, unfuckwithable, cared and rooted for.

Next, think of who you know, or who you imagine knowing, that would make you feel that way in their presence. Before you know it, in this example, I am "sitting at my dining table" with my team:

- Taylor Kitsch (from the *Friday Night Lights* years) is across from me, making it known with his strong and silent eye contact that he'll fuck up literally anyone who messes with me.
- Idris Elba is standing behind me and rubbing my shoulders, keeping me calm and grounded, and making me feel protected.
- Dwayne Johnson is sitting to my left, smiling and not saying a word as if his presence is so powerfully intimidating that as long as he's there, I am confident no one will mess with me, like ever, and that alone brings my internal and emotional safety back to a healthy, grounded place.
- John Krasinski (of course) is calmly sitting to my right, cracking dry one-liners and making faces when someone on the other end of the line says something mean or asshole-ish, which immediately removes the heaviness from the situation and brings a renewed sense of levity.

And you know what?
It works.
Pinky swear, it is the ultimate mindset hack when you are physically alone. By getting super clear on *how* you want to feel, then getting super

clear on what qualities of others would allow you to feel like you're in the safe protection of another, plus backing it up with a lucid daydream of anyone and everyone who can make that your perceived reality, it thus *becomes* your reality. At least from an emotional-intimacy perspective.

Which, for now, is enough.

And suddenly those difficult phone calls or the potentially high conflict in-person encounters (because you *know* my team comes with me to those as well) don't feel quite so difficult anymore because, baby, I don't *feel* so alone anymore.

Isn't that fascinating?
I am alone . . . I just don't *feel* alone.

Then there are the events, things like religious holidays/celebrations, Mother's Day, birthdays, significant anniversaries of past events . . . that can feel *very* heavy if you're looking at the calendar and realizing that once again you are, in fact, physically alone.

Being able to know and honor that about yourself allows you to be present with it as your current reality without judging or shaming it. You can choose to simply accept that there are significant events that, if left unattended to, will cause grief, and you can prepare for them well in advance.

Drawing from samples in my own life, Mother's Day stands out as one that is potentially rife with painful reminders that my life (and certainly our family life) does not look like I imagined. Yet.

I loop my kids in to help: I get clear on what I would really like to do and what feels manageable within any given circumstance, and I ask for their help. They like to bring breakfast (and coffee, bless them) with a little flower vase to me in bed, so a couple weeks before, I remind them and ask them to make a list of any supplies they may need. Then they "memory charm" me so I'll "forget" the specifics, and honestly, it feels like a surprise on Sunday morning when croissants toasted with Nutella and a giant mug of coffee with oat milk appear in my bed on a wooden serving tray held by little oven-mitted-clad hands.

Another example is my fortieth birthday, which happened during COVID-19. In knowing that I'd need to find a way of marking what felt like a special and sacred milestone in the timeline of my own life and being unable to physically be with anyone including my extended family during a stay-at-home order, I planned ahead.

Although I didn't have my girls scheduled to be with me that day, I asked their dad well in advance if I could have them home for dinner. We had a taco party with cupcakes in our backyard, and after I dropped them back at their dad's, I caught a sunset on the beach, played guitar, and sipped zero-alcohol sparkling rosé with strawberries.

It. Was. Heaven.

For both of those events, I sat with my girlies at my laptop, showing them what "they were getting me" as I ordered gold hoop earrings and the entire *Friday Night Lights* collection on DVD. I told them when the packages from Mejuri and Amazon arrived that they'd know what was inside.

And indeed, when those packages arrived, the girlies whisked them away, wrapped them, and gave them to me on the actual day of the event. In no way did I feel alone; I felt loved, seen, and cared for.

Each of these moments, each of which have *great potential* to be highly upsetting or triggering events, now feels special in its own unique way. Personally, I find them even more special because it feels so intentional to create such an honest level of preciousness. A little communication, planning, and clarity on *what feels good* will take you far.

In each of those moments/events/instances, all it does is solidify the feeling that while you *are* alone, you don't *feel* alone. And you don't feel so alone anymore because what you're really doing is not learning how to clap with one hand—you're learning how to play a different song entirely. It's cultivating the feeling that you belong to yourself.

Because when you belong to yourself, the truth and beauty of it is that you are never really alone.

CHAPTER THIRTEEN

ALONE IN PARENTING

During my first pregnancy, I came across a baby hammock. I was smitten. This thing, the philosophy behind which was to create a natural simulation of the movement of the womb and thereby making it a smooth and peaceful transition for your baby to sleep and feel safe, was the coolest baby thing I'd ever seen.

You could hang it beside your bed, making it easier to nurse, you could detach it and hang it in a tree, making it easy to have a life, and if your ever-understanding in-laws were as supportive as mine were, you could hang it on the giant eye hook they installed in "your" room at their house, making it easy to travel.

I became evangelical about this thing. Like most first-time parents, I felt deeply that I was *the* first person to ever have a baby and that naturally, having read all the right books (yet having no hands-on experience of my own), I was the preeminent expert.

What a treat this phase of life is for other people around us. LOL.

I was *desperate* to raise kids in opposition to how I'd been raised, meaning my intention was always to be loving, accepting, present, and supportive of doing whatever it took to give them the absolute best chance in life. I stand behind that now.

At the time, the best way I knew how to go about doing that was to read every book written that supported my Montessori-rooted beliefs in parenting as naturally as possibly: baby wearing, nursing, attachment parenting, co-sleeping, all in an attempt to make this little one feel ultra-safe and loved. I was openly anti-crib, anti-stroller, anti-anything-but-one-parent-needs-to-stay-at-home . . .

. . . and it worked.

Until twenty months later when I had twins.

Suddenly a home birth wasn't an option. I was medically mandated to have an ob-gyn, not a midwife, as my primary caregiver. Baby wearing wasn't physically possible, although for the first couple weeks of their young lives I did put both of them in one carrier for a while, then literally walked around my house with a baby on each hip—for months—after that.

Otherwise, now with three kids under two, I'd pop my toddler in the front of the stroller, then put one baby in the bottom and one baby in my carrier, making sure to alternate each one for equal amounts of time until I realized that neither of them really even *liked* the baby carrier.

Why? Because every child—and their needs—is different.

Suddenly attachment parenting and co-sleeping weren't possible because where my firstborn was like a Cadillac sleeper if she was in bed next to me, both of us sleeping smoothly and soundly, my twinsies squirmed uncomfortably around me. And when I put them in the hammock, I made it worse. I had to buy two cribs, one for each of them, in order to ensure their physical safety and teach them to sleep through the night—for their well-being and my own personal sanity.

Why? Because every child—and their needs—is different.

Suddenly even nursing became hella stressful. With my firstborn, I converted my wardrobe so I had exclusively nursing tops with a little flap of fabric I could pop up for easy access, and I nursed her with ease and discretion on the streetcar, at a family gathering in Amsterdam, on the freaking plane *to* Amsterdam that I took solo with my three-month-old, and at my kitchen bar during a dinner party I was hosting . . . without my friends even noticing. I was like a nursing ninja.

Nursing twins, however? See ya never, ninja skills.

Nursing twins, something I was passionate about, required "tandem nursing." If I wanted them to sleep at the same time, I needed to nurse them at the same time. Cut to me never leaving my house for about a year. I sat on the couch with one baby nestled in my left elbow, the other nestled on her sister's tummy as a pillow, then switched it up. It worked, and I am so glad I did it, but it was an entirely different experience from the first time around.

Why? Because every child—and their needs—is different.

Here's the truth no one really tells you about parenting, until one day it just dawns on you that it *is* the truth: *Everyone* is just figuring it out as they go in parenting—as in life.

- You can "do everything right" and end up with kids who are assholes or who, devastatingly, become addicted, estranged, or worse.
- You can "do everything wrong" and end up with kids who are incredible humans who, in spite of everything, find a way to persevere and overcome.

Despite what most (not all, but many) parenting coaches will try to sell you, there isn't one surefire way to raise healthy, well-adjusted kids.

Why? Because every child—and their needs—is different.

Remember that we talked about how humans aren't algorithms? That applies here too.

Yes, of course it is more likely that if you are present, accepting, engaged, and loving with your children, they will grow up to be healthy, well-adjusted kids. And personally, I believe *those* are the descriptors of parenting: to *be* present, accepting, engaged, and loving. It is what most of us are striving for.

And still, it isn't a "if you do this, then that will happen" equation because again, *every child—and their needs—is different*, and humans aren't algorithms.

The reality is that parenting is a different experience for everyone because everyone is different, which can often make it feel like an incredibly isolating experience. Yes, there are milestones, and yes, those are almost universally shared, yet still, the reality is that parenting, and raising a family, is an experience in which we are technically alone because of how unique those interfamily dynamics are.

On top of that, each new phase of childhood demands a new phase of parenting (any parent of toddlers or teens will feel this deeply). That constant "rebirth" process demands our constant adaption to a new skill set that we are (usually) unprepared for, which feels like a further isolating experience because it feels like you are constantly starting over and relearning everything you knew about your child, grieving the loss of the child they just were—like 10 minutes ago—as you go.

We each come into parenting carrying our own unique set of baggage, and if you are reading this book without having kids of your own, spoiler alert: It's usually having your own kids that forces you to haul all the old baggage out of your emotional basement and carefully reexamine every single piece you've collected in the past few decades.

Almost all my clients (or friends) who aren't yet in the mode of having kids but want to be, communicate that they want to heal all their shit now so they don't project it onto their children. I respect that so much— the self-awareness and commitment thereto that motivates them to heal it now, and as I tell each of them, while that is a noble and genuine intention, even when they've done a lot of healing on their own, most people have a whole new layer of *stuff* that bubbles up to the surface when they have or adopt kids because it forces them to reexamine life and their role in it in a different way.

That's not to say that people who choose not to have kids don't have this experience; they have their own stuff bubble up when the time is "right." I'm merely stating that parenting becomes an accelerated masterclass in sorting through and unpacking your own baggage.

That unpacking process alone can make parenting feel even more isolating because our own unique experience informs the wounds and intentions we have with respect to raising our own families. "I would *never* do this to my kids because it felt so awful; *this* was such an amazing part of my childhood that I can't *wait* to give it to my own kids."

We're all projecting because we're all mirrors of experience for one another, and since we are each technically still kids, even if we're taller and have mortgages and are allowed to eat ten Oreos before dinner, we—and our needs—are all different, which, in turn, makes the experience uniquely ours.

Fast-forward through our own childhood baggage to the life we're living now, and layer in all of the expectations versus reality:

- what we *thought* our partner would be like as a parent versus how they *are*
- what we *thought* parenting would be like versus how it *is*
- what we *thought* staying at home (or working outside of it) would be like versus how it *is*
- add your own—there's a myriad of unrequited expectations from which to choose

All of a sudden we realize this life we signed up for, this thing we've wanted for so long, or felt pressured into, or invested tens of thousands of dollars and months or years of time in IVF for, is wildly different than the one we were sold while watching TV.

Even the good stuff! That really good stuff that sneaks up on you in moments of joy, moments that all but erase the hard days or weeks that came before, moments you just want to shout from the rooftops, "Oh my gawwwwwd, this kid is amazing! Can you believe she just . . ." and then you realize that that moment, that deeply joyful moment, isn't as significant to anyone else but you because of how quiet and subtle and contextually special it is.

The days sometime seem to never end, but the years go by in an instant. The expertise you had in one area of your life seems to have no relevance to count toward parenting.
The community you once had is now separated by their own unique family circumstances.

You're Just. So. Tired.

You look around to ask a grown-up for help in figuring out the next challenge, only to realize that *you are the grown-up now.*

It's incredibly emotionally draining, boring (sorry, but it's true), and often equally as isolating.

Your work requires focus and awareness 24/7, for decades at a time, with no pay and minimal-to-no thanks for years or even decades at a time.

And the best metric of a job well done?

This little person you've invested all your time and love and energy into . . . leaves.

So, yeah. A lot of the time it feels like you are alone in parenting because a lot of the time you *are* alone in parenting.

The paradox? While each of our experiences in the day to day is unique, just like so much of our human experience, we are all sharing a common emotional experience *in* our feelings of alone-ness, isolation, uncertainty, and holy shit am I doing this right? What if I fuck it up?

And I don't know about you, but the knowledge that we share a common emotional experience makes it a little less isolating. Seeing it through the lens of *this is just what parenting feels like* is what allows us to feel so much less alone in wondering if this is, in fact, what this is supposed to feel like.

We already know that everything we see on TV is fake, thus setting us up for disappointment (and the subsequent buying of things to make us feel better). So, a lot of those perfect little families you see on TV? F.a.k.e. Real families don't make for great TV because real family life is often tedious with the best kind of boring punctuated by those moments of outrageous, but contextual, joy.

We also know that if the end is really the beginning, and that if *we* are all here for a specific purpose while learning specific lessons along the way, it stands to reason that each of our children is also here for a specific purpose while learning specific lessons along the way.

Add to that what we know about walking our own unique path to learn those lessons and explore that purpose and suddenly the job of parenting feels a little more freeing and a lot less isolating because in raising these tiny humans, we are each far more connected to the bigger picture than we may have thought.

The job of parenting *isn't* to raise perfect kids who get into the right colleges and land the right jobs and make the right amount of money.

The job of parenting *isn't* to be a hard-ass who is respected and feared as the omniscient expert of the family, nor is it to be a human game of curling by sweeping the ice clear of any obstacles so that little rock can sail forward and never encounter adversity.

The job of parenting is to be the tour guide of your child's life, to use your own acquired skills and lessons to facilitate and support your child's travels along their own unique path.

Your child is not your friend or confidant.

Your child is not an extension of you.

Your child is not your identity.

Your child is not your partner.

Your child is not the opportunity to relive an experience or to live vicariously through one.

Your child is not a project of your creation.

Your child is not a metric of your success or achievement.

Your child (and each of your children) is a part of your own experiential learning and is in your charge to lovingly guide along the many ups, downs, twists, and turns of your respective paths for as long as they overlap and with as much tenderness and wisdom as is mutually possible along the way.

It is that simple; it is that complicated.

When you can let go of the need for perfection as a reflection of who you are, when you can love and accept each one of your children as the unique individuals they are, when you can appreciate that you are not entitled to anything from them except the chance to choose presence, learning, and love at every opportunity, you are actively engaged in teaching your child what it means to belong.

That teaching process of what it means to belong begins on your own unique path as you cultivate exactly what that belonging looks and feels like, starting with how to belong to yourself.

Because when you belong to yourself, the truth and beauty of it is that you are never really alone.

CHAPTER FOURTEEN

ALONE IN OUR WORK

The first billionaire I ever met had one arm, wore a fur coat, and drove a Ferrari. Sitting across from him at the birthday dinner where we met for a mutual connection, I drunkenly and naïvely asked him what I didn't know I didn't know about transitioning my then teaching career into something—anything—else in the working world.

He looked at me very earnestly and told me the key was that "business" was its own language, and if I could learn to speak the language of business, I'd have everything I need.

The second billionaire I met lived part time on his vineyard, overlooking the river in the most beautiful part of Canada I have ever seen. He was a shipping magnate who'd made his money through—wait for it—lentils.

Once again, drunk and naïve, I asked him what I didn't know I didn't know about transitioning my teaching career into something—anything—else in the working world.

He looked at me very earnestly and told me the key was that if you want to make a lot of money, like a *lot* a lot of money, you find one teeny tiny almost insignificant thing and sell a shit ton of it.

Before I accidentally started my business, I had a habit of getting drunk and asking the right people the wrong questions about what I didn't know I didn't know. And over the years, I've looked back at each of the little clues they gave me and noted that almost all of them were a variation of the same things: learning the language gets you a seat at the table; make one thing and replicate it a billion times; you'll never make money working for someone else; the stock market always, *always*, goes up.

All of it made sense, and the business coaches I've worked with have supported it all to be true while deifying the earning potential of passive income, and . . .
None of it has ever resonated with me, specifically.

And for me personally, for a long time, that made me feel like I was alone in entrepreneurship too, like there was a club of people who "got it," and because I could "get it" but really not connect with it, or see the point, I felt like I couldn't sit at that table.

There is a notion in entrepreneurship, and particularly in female-owned online entrepreneurship, I have found, that there is a one-size-fits-all model to follow, and if your dream doesn't scare you, it's not big enough. In reality?

That is a lie.

Entrepreneurs are not followers who use someone else's roadmap to success.
True entrepreneurs are:

- Dreamers
- Doers
- Painfully aware that there is an infinite loop of niches in need and desire who are waiting for just the right thing that speaks to them in just the right way.
- Completely unaware that there even *is* a box, let alone think outside of it; they're off somewhere else entirely, figuring out how to turn their own unique vision into their own unique reality and wondering how the hell it's possible that nobody has done it yet.
- Just a little dash of crazy.

And that?
That secret sauce made of equal parts passion, intellect, and insanity?

That isn't scalable. It isn't replicable. It relies on its own language, while being well versed in a few others, in order to create what hasn't yet been created.

And that is a lonely, if rewarding, experience.

What about the ones who choose a more "traditional" path over entre-preneurship and focus on climbing the ladder from the bottom all the way up to the top? That climb that requires its own unique scope of focus, being able to strategize which move to make and when, who to rely on and why, how to get it done while getting noticed, and how to get noticed without standing out too much in the wrong way?

That is a lonely experience.

What about the ones who choose safety and security over the passion of entrepreneurship? Or the ones who follow the career path their parents envisioned for them? Or the ones who lock into a career that offers financial stability, then work only to maintain the lifestyle to which they become accustomed and subsequently feel beholden to the "golden handcuffs" of the multiple six-figure salary? Or the ones that feel as if they can't do anything other than what they've always done—even if what they've always done is, cough, soul-sucking work they don't enjoy?

That is a lonely experience.

Even in our work, no matter if it's rewarding emotionally or financially, or both, there is an element of feeling isolated and alone. And when we start to feel those icky feelings of isolation, loneliness, or that we don't really belong in the way we thought "belonging" would feel like in our professional lives, we reach for that old standby pattern of do, achieve, repeat.

And usually, it works: We do more, we get more—more clients, more money, more accolades. Our houses get bigger (and closer to the water), our cars get fancier (and more expensive), and our vacations become more lavish (and more exclusive).

And we create a lifestyle that is so rich that we have to stay hella rich to maintain it, which puts further pressure on us to perform, thus leaving us feeling more alone, depleted, and isolated from our families for whom we were really doing this all for anyway, and we wonder . . .

. . . how do we still feel alone?
. . . how can we have so much, but not feel like we thought we'd feel?
. . . whose metrics of success are we measuring ourselves against?
. . . how much is enough?
. . . what does enough even feel like?

Fighting your way to the top of whatever you're doing, only to look around and realize that holy shit, there's almost nobody there at your level, or who understands you, or who is rooting for you without feeling threatened by your success . . .

. . . *is its own fresh hell of loneliness.*

When you're in the building stages of whatever work you choose, it's a conscious decision to:

- Tune out the naysayers and haters in order to focus on realizing your own vision.
- Deliberately surround yourself with people who are more successful than you so you constantly feel motivated, inspired, and

driven to keep going beyond what you may have been told or even *believed* was possible for you.

- Put on those blinders and focus on the task at hand until the day comes when, once again, you realize *you did it* and now feel alone in your success.

It doesn't really feel fair, does it?

So, the temptation is to take that loneliness and channel it into our work even more to the extent that our work becomes more than an extension of us instead of feeling like it *is* us. We use work to keep us company, and we come enmeshed with our work as *who we* are instead of *what we do.*

Have you seen *Miss Americana*? The Taylor Swift documentary on Netflix?

Taylor describes the moment as she's walking to the stage about to receive her first Grammy (at such a young age—seventeen, I think?), and instead of feeling like "wow, I did it; I've been dreaming of this my whole life," her feelings were "oh shit, this is what I've been working toward, and now it's done. *What am I supposed to do next?*"

When we enmesh ourselves with our work, which is to say that we associate our work as fundamental to our identity, we start to also associate *the success of our work* with *the success of our identity.*

- If my business is thriving, I personally am thriving.
- If my work is being celebrated, I personally am being celebrated.

And that doesn't sound so bad until you get to the other side of the coin:

- If my business is failing, I personally am failing.
- If my work doesn't feel significant, I personally am not significant.

Entrepreneurs fall into this trap *all the time.*
Folks who follow a traditional career path fall into this trap *all the time.*

There's a sweet spot of being able to stand proudly in what you do without becoming beholden to it defining who you are because one day when you close your business, or feel the need to change career directions, or get laid off, or retire, it causes unnecessary loss of identity in what could otherwise be a regular part of life and the healthy transition in the liminal space from what was, through what is, to what will be.

The key is to learn how to clap for yourself.

In my first book, I wrote a chapter on the myth of competition, reframing it through the lens that because we are hardwired to belong to the group, we are hardwired to look around and see that what we are doing aligns with the group so as to feel like we are accepted and that we belong. I wrote about how *dumb* it is to compare yourself to anyone beyond that point of your hardware, because life only ever exists in moments, so to measure one moment of your own perceived success or failure against one moment of anyone else's perceived success or failure is futile. There will always be someone who is doing better than you, and there will always be someone who's doing worse.

Instead, what if we reframed the metrics of what success looks—and feels—like, and how to define those in a way you measure your work against them:

What are your values?

What are your dreams?

What is your purpose?

What unique qualities do you possess that you feel called to share?

How do you envision your lasting impact on the world to be?

How do you personally want to feel in and about your work?

What feelings do you want to create that your work will help facilitate or accommodate?

What does work-life blend or balance feel like for you?

One of the first coaches I worked with walked me through an "ideal day" exercise. I was asked what I would do for a year if money were no object. I thought about it, then said that I'd do exactly what I was doing, but I'd insert Mr. Wonderful into the picture. "No," she said. "What is your *dream*?"

Uh, this. I was living it. Except for Mr. Wonderful not yet being in the picture.

"NO!" she said. "You're not listening. What is your dreammmm*muh*?"

I think I told her, "Okay, fine, I'd move to Bali," just to shut down the conversation or appease her (my boundaries hadn't yet fully formed back then), but in reality, the idea of packing up kids and moving across the world sounded like a nightmare, not a dream.

My own personal dream is very similar to what Tolstoy wrote in *Family Happiness*:

"A quiet secluded life in the country, with the possibility of being useful to people to whom it is easy to do good, and who are not accustomed to have it done to them; then work which one hopes may be of some use; then rest, nature, books, music, love for one's neighbor—such is my idea of happiness."

My dream is so *simple* that it sometimes scares me, which is its own kind of feeling alone, and its own kind of freedom, but most importantly, it is a dream that 100 percent aligns with my values and vision of how I specifically want to feel in this lifetime.

In reality? Nobody really knows what feels right for you, except you.

The value in working with a (good) coach or mentor is to have someone ask you the right questions at the right times and listen to everything you're saying and, even better, listen to what you're *not* saying and then share the moments of highly contextual, subtle, but immensely powerful joy that come from doing what feels right and good for you.

That's where the magic starts to happen: when the little clues of what you actually want start to surface, and you can peel back the layers of personal, family, or intergenerational history that told you it's not okay to want what you want, and it certainly isn't okay to *have* what you want, or that having what you want is rife with conditions of love and acceptance.

Most (not all, but a lot of) business coaches can't take you deep enough in uncovering that because it falls outside the parameters of the formula and the algorithm we've been conditioned to follow, scale, and repeat.

But you already know now that humans aren't algorithms. This approach doesn't work with any longevity for most people because it isn't an authentic reflection of who they are. And that is true whether you're climbing a ladder or building your own: The long-game strategy of winning in your work—with winning being feeling deeply fulfilled by—is figuring out who you are and what you want.

Not who someone told you you are.
Not what someone told you you want.
Not because of what reward it's going to get you in the end.

Remember when I told you that each of us is going to die alone? Oof. That remains true no matter what is reflected on your bank statement, so you may as well make it count in the *qualitative* feeling of richness not just in the *quantitative* measurement of richness.

All of it starts by appreciating that feeling alone or even lonely in your work is also very human, and when you are aware of how human that is, you can start to have a little more self-compassion and a little less self-perfection and sink into the reality that even this is a shared emotional experience: We all feel this way, some more than others, for short to long periods of time in our working lives.

The key is to cultivate a sense of richness in doing what you love and loving what you do, being well and fairly compensated for that, and allowing space in your life for *living,* not just the working professional part of your life. That richness is cultivated through a keen sense of knowing what feels good, knowing what aligns with your values, and feeling neurologically and emotionally safe to take the necessary action to live your dream—your *specific* dream—and embody the feeling that all of it is an extension of the relationship you have with yourself. When that relationship is strong, even when you feel a little alone in your work life, you still feel like you belong to yourself.

And, of course, when you belong to yourself, the truth and beauty of it is that you are never really alone.

CHAPTER FIFTEEN

ALONE IN OUR SOCIAL LIVES

Early in the pandemic, when the first and global lockdown was happening, people all over the internet were lamenting how hard it was to not be able to go out and see their friends. Weekends, evenings, getaways, travel plans . . . all were canceled without warning and without any word of when we'd be able to resume "normal" life, however normal life would look.

There were waves of shock and waves of grief, even in the early days of this massive, worldwide event. And one day, it hit me like a hard truth with absolutely *no soft pillow* in sight:

My social life hadn't changed.
Almost at all.
Oof.

In the "before times" as a single, solo parent who lives in a small town of mostly elderly or married couples, my weekends were either spent with my girlies or doing a solo road trip, usually heading into Toronto for a day trip or evening out, or maybe a drive out to Prince Edward County, a really beautiful wine and food area on the lake just east of me, affectionately known as "The County." On occasion, I'd rent a small cabin or cool treehouse up north in Muskoka (think: Canadian Hamptons) on my own for a little escape or spend some time driving out to see my extended family for a couple of days.

Yes, all of *that* was canceled, and yes, that cancellation sucked. For months and months at a time.

And still, most of that social time was still time spent *by myself,* and the longing people spoke of to be with their friends again and to have the freedom to just go out when they wanted hit me hard because when the world slowed down and even stopped, it made me profoundly aware of how empty my immediate social circle is, which I think I'd denied until it was suddenly staring me in the face.

I felt alone in my social life.

That aloneness has sparked much sadness, longing, and *shame.*[4] The solitude of my life was exacerbated by the alone-ness and isolation of what felt like a never-ending pandemic. So, those parts that felt the

....

4 There was a time when those dark feelings would almost be *welcomed* in by the old, dark, and shadowy parts of my ego, the parts we all have that pop up every now and then to remind us that we're a fake, a failure, not enough.

sadness, shame, and longing quickly succumbed to the heaviness of feeling like a fake, a failure, not enough. It's not pretty.

How many of us felt that way?
How many of us got slapped in the face by how little had changed to our social life in the face of this global event and felt too ashamed to talk about it?

How can we reframe that feeling, that fear, without numbing it on the couch watching *The Office* (again) with a pint of pistachio gelato?

The reality is, in a particular season of life, we are maxed out for resources, and our friendships and social life are often the first things to go.

Work, parenting, infertility, care of parents, marriage, dating, getting divorced, breaking up, staying healthy, managing an illness, building a career, climbing the ladder, personal goal setting, reinventing . . . all require energy.

And to be in a friendship, a healthy and loving friendship, requires two people balancing and blending it all and still making time for each other while being respectful of boundaries and needs.

It's not an easy task. The investment of time, energy, and attention required to *be* a present and loving friend is real.

A few years ago, I was in what felt like *the* best friendship. Amy and I did e v e r y t h i n g together. We had the exact same sense of humor, loved all the same things, hated all the same things, had the same taste in music, loved vinyl and bourbon, enjoyed shopping for vintage jackets and going away for a weekend at the drop of a floppy BoHo hat because we could . . .

When we'd go out, we'd meet incredible people, get matching tattoos, and have the most magical experiences as if our collective energy as a duo drew people into our vortex of awesome. Awesome things happened All. The. Time. And when we'd drive back from the city or were turning in from a night out at the bar or day by the pool, she'd ask me to sing to her until she fell asleep.

No matter what we were doing, we were laughing our faces off all the time. We even travelled perfectly together.

I've never experienced anything like it before or since; it felt like the *totally nonsexual* relationship of my dreams. We were so in synch.

Her husband, too, was an *amazing* man. Charming, funny, low key, and completely supportive of anything either of us wanted to do. He was an actively listening shoulder to cry on for both of us, always went to pick up the takeout we ordered, came with me as my "date" to be a buffer in what was an otherwise painfully anxious yet necessary social event I had to go to, and was *so present* for my kids.

Amy and I got to know each other's families, and it felt like she was an actual sister; she loved my kids like an amazing aunt loves her nieces. She was engaged and involved in their lives and came to their school concerts with flowers. We went apple picking. We cut our family Christmas trees together. I went to family parties with her, went to her nephew's rugby game, and sat outside in her brother's backyard and watched the Tragically Hip's final concert on the TV rigged up outside.

Once, on our way into the city with my girlies for a photoshoot, one of my daughters threw up all over the backseat; my friend just cleaned it up while I comforted my daughter, and when we turned around to skip the shoot and go back home, Amy just patiently breathed out the window without ever reacting to the smell of vomit in my station wagon.

And once, on my way back home from a road trip to the Midwest, I met up with her brother Matt for lunch at one of those "Tollway Oasis" island rest stops they have in Illinois, talked for hours, and drove the rest of the way home imagining what it would be like when he and I got married and Amy and I *actually* became sisters.

It all burned so hot, so fast, and it really felt like we were the family the other had been searching for. It was the relationship of my dreams—the totally nonsexual friendship version.

Most of all, it just felt so intimately connected, safe, joyful, and fun. It was heaven.

Then we went to Chicago for a few days to celebrate New Year's Eve. Amy asked me a direct question while we were putting on mascara just before we went out, I gave her a direct answer with honesty and with what I thought was tenderness in my honesty, and I really hurt her feelings.

Lashing out, she said a stream of things that were so raw that it felt like she'd been feeling *that* all the time without telling me, and that really hurt *my* feelings. It felt like something had snapped inside her, revealed how she really felt, which made something snap inside me, knowing how she really felt.

We had both violated unspoken conditions of what was and was not acceptable to each of us, we had not respected the boundaries we had each silently put in place, and the damage was done. Less than two weeks later, that friendship was over. I never heard from her (or her husband) again. It was painful . . . and also freeing.

In hindsight, the intense friendship we had, while rich in so many magical moments that I still look back on now and can laugh out loud about within minutes, was *highly* codependent in nature.

Each of us had had *significant* unresolved trauma from our past, and our friendship became a safe haven for living out the freedom of a wildly playful childhood neither of us ever had until our adult selves caught up with us and made us each examine what was really going on.

And what was really going on was that we had become so enmeshed in each other's lives that we'd lost our independent sense of self, and neither had space to breathe independently; *we had unwittingly and accidentally suffocated our relationship.*

Can you relate?

You know unconditional love is largely a myth: Everyone has conditions and boundaries on what it means to be in a relationship with us, including a friendship, and when those boundaries are violated or the conditions are unmet, it kills the love.

When I called time of death on my marriage, I violated an unknown condition of many of the friendships I'd had when I was coupled. And when 99 percent of those friends chose to hang out with and support my ex after the fact? It absolutely violated all kinds of conditions of my love and trust.

Violating those conditions, aka boundaries, is a real thing and is often a deal breaker in any number of relationships. As someone who is chronically on time (because if you're not five minutes early, you're ten minutes late), I've had friends in the past with whom I have communicated, "When you say you will be there at 8:00, then consistently show up at 9:30 without any apology or context, it makes me feel like you don't care about me" only to have them show up even later the next time we hang out? That's a boundary violation for me, and the friendship fizzles out.

Can you relate?

I've had friends in the past get really curious about my work and the specific details thereof. They ask for a step-by-step account of what I've done and how, then ask to be connected with my carefully curated network. Conscious of being an attentive and supportive friend, I've often shared that information. And magically, when I stop sharing that information, or when I've gently but clearly communicated that it feels more like an unpaid coaching or mentorship relationship, my phone stops ringing at just about the same time my friend's business is taking off in its new direction.

It sucks. *So much.*

Can you relate?

We don't talk about the pain over the endings of friendships; we talk about breakups with romantic partners, but we seldom talk about the breakup of friendships, and I can't figure out why that is. I think it harkens back to having some pretty lofty expectations of what friendship is supposed to be like, and so we cling to that largely unrequited dream and stay in friendships that feel draining, one sided, unsupportive, or otherwise toxic because it's as if we don't know we're allowed to leave the friendships that don't serve us.

It's as if we'd rather stay in friendships that don't really work because we don't want to be alone.

Friendships are an energy investment. And when your energy is already spread thin across all the areas of your life in which you are committed to investing that energy, friendship can fall by the wayside.

Having been burned by so many people I had previously called friends in my life and having had the boundaries of my love and trust repeatedly violated, I am now pretty conscious of with whom I share that energy at a friendship level.

In those early and dark days of the pandemic that brought all the old fears out to play, I had a subtle but powerful realization: *maybe this just wasn't the friendship season of my life.* Maybe this was the season that demanded I be present in my family, present in my business, present in healing my body after cancer, present in healing my heart from trauma—and learning to feel consistently safe in that healed place without waiting for the other shoe to drop.

Maybe this was the season I just needed to be present for *me* and *let that be what it is.*

Mark Twain said, "The worst loneliness is not to be comfortable with yourself," and he was right: getting comfortable with who you are and investing the necessary time and attention in *that* relationship, even if the timing of that relationship doesn't align with your vision of what you thought it would or should be like, is the foundation on which we build all other relationships.

What if you're in the season of life that doesn't allow you to *be* a present or loving friend right now? What if, instead of shaming that, we could really own the energy demands life has on us and find peace in being friendly—and kind, of course—and being honest with the people we love who we have a finite amount of time to be in a reciprocal friendship with . . . and let that be enough?

Some of my closest friends, the ones I know I can rely on and who can rely on me without ever *over expecting* anything from each other, are the ones *I hardly see socially.* Most of them don't live in the same town as I do, or even the same country. One of my closest friends lives more than a thousand miles from me in Milwaukee and is a go-to, trusted confident. We met at a retreat years ago and have only seen each other in person once after that, when we did our NLP Practitioner training together. And still? The distance doesn't affect our emotional closeness.

My closest friends and I are there for each other without question when we need it, but we seldom, if ever, get together and hang out.

For example, I once sent a frantic text to a friend I don't hang out with very often because of the seasons of life we're both in as parents, people, and entrepreneurs. I told her I'd had sex with a tampon in and now the laws of physics and *great sex* had made that tampon inaccessible to me, and what the hell was I supposed to do?

Hand to God, she arrived at my place ten minutes later, told me to lie down on my bed and take a breath, reached in and *pulled the fucking sex tampon* out of my vagina. I don't care what Hollywood says friendship looks like, that act right there is the sign of a true friend: that one intimate moment of 100 percent trust and zero percent judgment *communicated more* in less than thirty seconds total than any number of lunches, nights out, or weekends away ever could.

It's really important to factor in quality over quantity when we're talking about our friendships and social lives because this is a complicated and demanding season of life. This season of life just doesn't have enough bandwidth to be everything to everyone; remember, you can have it all . . . maybe just not at the same time.

We don't like to talk about it, but *one is not the loneliest number*; if you don't feel comfortable or secure being who you are, what is it that you're bringing with you to your social life and friendships? What boundaries are missing that allow those around you to take advantage of you and drain all your energy?

Pay attention to how you feel when you leave parties, gatherings, nights out—hell, Zoom calls: Are the people you're spending time with leaving you feeling light, lifted, supported, and joyful? Or is there a sense of anxiousness, heaviness, needing to sleep for an hour just to come back from that social interaction?

Be protective of your energy.
Be mindful of your boundaries.
Be conscious of what demands your time and commitment and how much of that feels free and fun and how much of that feels like obligation or fear of disappointing someone else.

When you are clear on each of those, you are cultivating a deeper relationship, and friendship, with yourself. That is the relationship that will, over time, attract the right people into your life because it is the one that is healthy, respectful, loving, and makes you unequivocally aware that you belong.

Because when you belong to yourself, the truth and beauty of it is that you are never really alone.

CHAPTER SIXTEEN

ALONE IN OUR GRIEF

I had a miscarriage in my early thirties.

I was only about eight weeks into my pregnancy, and while I knew the stats that one in four pregnancies end in miscarriage, I never thought mine would be one of the four, nor did I anticipate what a *devastating* loss it would feel like, that early on.

When you know, you know.

I remember sitting at my kitchen counter, two weeks later in yoga pants and a black-and-white striped long-sleeved tee, literally doubled over in grief. It felt like my soul was weeping and grieving the loss of a little one I didn't even know; a primal place inside of me that was beyond my control was absolutely stricken with grief. My then-husband came in, asked me what was wrong, and when I looked up from my now snot-covered arms where I'd been resting my head and crying, I said, "I *had* a *MISCARRIAGE*," and he said, "Oh, are you still upset about that?"

We had experienced the same loss, yet we didn't experience the same *grief* of that loss in remotely the same way.

I think that's a common feeling after tragedy: Even when we share a collective experience of loss, *we experience our grief so differently* that it feels incredibly isolating and like we are completely alone in that grief.

When my little sister died suddenly at age twenty-one while away on vacation, our immediate family, which already had a complex relational dynamic (to put it lightly), experienced a shared loss, but we were each alone in our grieving. I felt so excluded from being able to grieve *with* my family; it felt like my grief and grief management didn't meet their expectations of what my grief *should* look like.

We had experienced the same loss, yet didn't experience the same *grief* of that loss in remotely the same way.

And in that experience, I know I'm not alone.

Our grief is not linear.
And neither is our healing.

It's not the nice and tidy five-step process laid out by Kübler-Ross in the late sixties that suggests we move through grief one stage at a time, starting with denial and passing through anger, bargaining, and depression before arriving ultimately at acceptance.

Nope.

As anyone who's ever experienced loss and the grief brought on by that loss will tell you, our grief, and every stage of that grief, unfolds in layers and comes in waves, each one hitting us when we least expect it and often when everything else in our life feels good, if not great.

For example, when you're stopped at a red light, singing away to your playlist, and a song comes on that reminds you of *what happened* and then you're a puddle. Or my other personal favorite: when you're shopping in the cereal aisle and are overcome by a wave of grief for which you can't even identify the triggering source. It just . . . appears.

I wrote in my first book that if we imagine our one Self composed of many, many selves all healing toward an integrated whole, as we heal one part of our Self, we make it neurologically and emotionally safe enough for us to heal *another* part of our Self, which is a really good thing!

It's also why the healing process—and I am talking about the *deep* healing process—can feel more like "Are we there yet? Are you fucking kidding me? How much more healing needs to happen before I can just feel *whole*?"

I get it.

To say "it's frustrating" is an understatement. And even though every time we reach a new level of healing, it truly is bringing us a deeper and more integrated feeling of wholeness, it still hurts, thus returning us to the very Buddhist notion that life effectively *is* suffering, and one of our tasks in this life is to learn how to manage that suffering by being present in moments, appreciating the fleeting nature of those moments, choosing to see the One-ness of us all, and trusting love as the great connector while we ebb and flow with the waves of emotion and without judgment of that emotion.

But still.

It hurts.

Much of our pain doesn't come from the experience of what happened, it comes from our perceived inability to *talk about* the experience of what happened.

Personally, I lived it firsthand throughout several traumatic experiences in my own life, from abuse, to divorce, to cancer. It felt as if some losses (and traumas) were socially acceptable to talk about (like cancer), which helped make it relatively easy to process as an experience.

But the other experiences that felt less socially acceptable to talk about and therefore more taboo (like abuse and divorce) made them very difficult to process because I felt like I had to hide my experience and loss, plus hide my feelings about that loss, which wrapped the whole thing in a heavy wet blanket of shame.

Professionally, I see it *each and every time I work with a private client* who starts our call with a feeling of overwhelm, or like they need to hide or diminish their experience and feelings born from that experience, and then by the end of our session, feels a renewed sense of energy, clarity, confidence, courage, and hope, often describing these feelings as a lightness in their chest or heart.

Therein lies the value of mentorship and good therapeutic coaching: It's a sacred container designed to bear judgment-free witness to your experience and help heal you forward by processing your actual feelings that come from that experience.

It's so beautiful to witness people step into reclaiming ownership of their story, experience, and life in this way, simply by sharing their honest feelings and letting someone else help shoulder that pain of everyday life.

Because it isn't just the major or "capital T Trauma" life events that come with the layered heaviness of grief. It isn't just death, divorce, illness, economic hardship, fear thereof, or hey, a pandemic that gives you all of that *and more* in one giant serving.

It's the concentric rings of loss that stem from each of those experiences.

It's the quieter, more subtle layers of loss that come from grieving *unrequited expectations and opportunities* we thought we'd have.

It's the coming-of-age awareness that *this life ends*, and with it the awareness that it doesn't feel like you've *quite* finished setting out what you had hoped to do.

It's the *loss of the vision* you had for your life, the *loss of the feeling* you thought you'd find in one place until you realize you were looking in the wrong place, and now you've *lost that time* spent searching for something that wasn't there.

It's the natural *loss of one phase of life* (including how your body looks, moves, and feels) as you transition, or watch dear ones transition, that you didn't expect to be over so soon, and it's the *loss of all the teeny tiny things you didn't know you loved* and took for granted until you wake up one morning and realize they're gone.

Hard truth, soft pillow: Life is suffering.
How we choose to process that suffering is up to us, and it lies solely within our control to do so.

When we choose to keep that suffering to ourselves, we do so largely because we feel like our experience doesn't count, like our loss isn't big enough, especially compared to what other people have endured, and therefore, our loss and subsequent grief don't really matter.

It matters.

Your story matters.
Your experience matters.
Your feelings matter.

Your pain is your pain, and all pain is relative.

When we choose to share that suffering with the right people in the right context with the right boundaries, our suffering doesn't necessarily melt away, or even go away entirely, but it does lift, and it does let us know that we are safe to let others into our hearts, which makes us feel less alone.

There is emphasis on the "right people in the right context with the right boundaries" here. Inviting in the wrong people in the wrong context with the wrong boundaries won't lift you up or make you feel seen and heard and held—it'll make you feel drained, depleted, and lost.

Have you ever watched *Breaking Bad*, aka one of the greatest shows that has ever and will ever be made? There's a scene in which Jesse (the unwitting protagonist) is in the depths of significant loss. And grief. And guilt. And shame.

As a coping mechanism to *not confront* any of those feelings and shadows, he opens his house to become a twenty-four-hour party. The music is aggressively loud. The house is packed with people dancing, drugging, fucking, and passing out. It's shot hyper-lapsed so you see all the mayhem happening around Jesse who is sitting alone on the floor in the corner, drowning it all out while avoiding his own grief.

He surrounds himself in distractions to deliberately avoid being in his pain.
We call that "bypassing."

Bypassing also looks like:

- turning to drugs, booze, risky sexual encounters, and excessive shopping/eating/exercising
- being overly positive even in the pit of your own grief with "good vibes only" tropes
- over-spiritualizing the experience without confronting your true feelings

Looking for (healthy) coping mechanisms isn't a bad thing.
Looking for optimism isn't a bad thing.
Looking for the bigger picture isn't a bad thing.
All of that, when in balance, is actually a *great thing.*

But keeping each of those in balance starts with *feeling* your feelings in a deeply honest way.

When you can be honest with yourself about what you're feeling, that's when you can also be honest with yourself about eventually being able to process how this weaves itself into your plan. Onto your path. How it's a part of your whole, and how your whole is a part of the collective whole.

COVID-19 and the concentric rings of loss of life it incurred not only from the virus itself but also the loss of life as we knew it, the loss of the *illusion* that people had equal rights in what many thought *was* a socially just Western world that had ended racism back in the sixties, the loss of trust in our leadership, the loss of faith in so many areas of humanity, the loss of trust in the news and dissemination of truth and information, and the loss of physical connections, just to name a few, didn't just affect us as individuals, it affected us as a global community.

I personally *loathed* the rhetoric that "we're all in this together," because we're not: the 1 percent had and is having a much different experience than the 99 percent, and within that 99 percent are *tiers* of privilege and the absence thereof. However, the one thing that we do share, regardless of geography or age or social status, is loss, which, like pain, is completely relative.

The loss was personal, but the grief was collective, and it likely will be for some time.

So, the question becomes—with respect to the many losses we have and will incur in our lives—how do we:

- experience loss as individuals *and*
- process grief personally and as part of a collective *and*
- feel the full depths of our experience *and*
- not become trapped in or beholden to the pain of our story?

Ain't that the million-dollar question?

Very simply, it's a matter of choosing both/and instead of the either/or we are so often conditioned to choose.

Choose to both feel your feelings *and* feel free to move on.
Choose to both experience your grief *and* allow yourself to experience joy.
Choose to both have compassion for yourself and others *and* set appropriate boundaries therein.
Choose to both allow your story to inform your present *and* not let it define your future.

Any loss feels like death. In fact, some losses can feel even harder than death when we don't get the finality and closure that a physical death brings. When it's a metaphorical death, like the death of a marriage, friendship, dream, or expectation, it sometimes feels like we're living in this zombie world in which that person or thing is dead to *us* but is very much alive and living their own life or existence just out of arm's reach from us.

In each or any of those deaths, so much of our grief comes from being in the liminal space of what was, what is, and what is yet to be. That's a complex state of feeling for a brain that is programmed for certainty and derives safety from what is known.

We know what we knew, and we don't yet know what we'll know. Which sucks.

It sucks, even when we know that we're each walking our own path, at our own pace, as a part of our plan, and that divine timing of that process pretty much never makes sense at the time, and sometimes never makes sense, or *ever* feels fair.

Choosing to allow yourself to experience and process the full range of your emotions allows you to be in both/and, and that is what allows you to safely cultivate the feeling that you are not alone in your experience and that you are, in fact, sharing a human experience even if you never meet someone who seems like they're sharing the experience with you. Inviting the right people in at the right time with whom you trust to bear witness to your experience and grief is a massive step in your own self-trust.

Trusting yourself is a massive step in cultivating the reality that you belong to yourself.

And when you belong to yourself, the truth and beauty of it is that you are never really alone.

PART THREE: COURAGE

CHAPTER SEVENTEEN

IN THE MEANTIME

I live in a small town with a great beach; one of my favorite hobbies is to drive to an even smaller town, with an even better beach, to catch the sunset. I bring my peppermint tea and a Mexican or Indigenous blanket and camp out on an enormous piece of driftwood to watch the sun go down.

It's heavenly.

One day I went out midafternoon (to what often feels like my own private beach), and I brought my three girlies with me for a beach walk. At first, they were annoyed because they thought our beach walk meant walking many miles of beachfront, and so the three of them ran up ahead of me so they could commiserate in their annoyed-ness.

There I was on this spectacular spring day, the kind that feels like early summer, with all of the sun and none of the humidity. I took off my shoes and walked barefoot in the sand along the shore. As I walked, I found myself focusing on where I was stepping in that moment because the shoreline of this particular beach has its own fair share of rocks. So, as I walked barefoot, I, too, started getting annoyed because I kept hurting my feet on rocks and shells. And when I walked closer to the water, the ankles of my linen pants started getting wet, and that felt annoying, and the time I wanted to have with my kids wasn't happening because they were walking up ahead. Then those stupid little cluster bugs kept zooming at my face and one got in my mouth, then another one got in my eyelashes and . . .

. . . I paused.

I could feel myself getting stressed out—while walking on the *beach*, for heaven's sake.

I took a breath and looked up, realizing I'd only been focusing on walking where I was, one step at a time, looking for things that could hurt me.

I shifted my gaze ever so slightly toward the horizon, and I suddenly saw what I'd been intending to find but in reality, I had been missing:

- It was a beautiful day.
- I was out in nature along a gorgeous beach.
- My three kids were having their own sweet sister time, talking about who knows what but laughing and just *be*ing together.
- I was . . . happy.

A little laugh and huge smile came across my face: I had been so busy looking at where I was that I had completely lost sight of what was happening around me and where I was going.

I thought about *what a pleasure it was to be in that moment right then.*

I let the hems of my pants get wet. I kept my eyes on the horizon so I could fully appreciate the glory and freedom of where I was.
I looked forward to see where I was going, beyond this moment, and if my feet stepped on a rock or a miniature bug flew into my mouth every now and then?

Meh. It really wasn't so bad.

And I got to thinking about what a necessary metaphor for life this experience was.

Being present is crucial to your mental and emotional health and wellness. But choosing to be present doesn't mean losing sight of where you're headed overall or getting wrapped up in the often-excruciating minutia of where you are.

In fact, choosing to be present, fully present, means to *savor* the experience of your present moment *without judging* the experience of your present moment.

Feeling the proverbial sand under your feet. Sun on your face. Water lapping at your ankles. What a pleasure it is to be in this moment of your life and embracing it exactly as it is while also being aware that there is so much more on the horizon that you have yet to experience.

That balance—in between the lines of that liminal space in which you dance your way from what was, through what is, to what will be—is often a tough one to strike.

Chances are that if you are feeling significantly alone, in one or more of the areas that we've explored so far, I am willing to bet that you're feeling or have recently felt the burn of this season of your life. And I'm willing to bet that if those feelings are present, even if you know in your heart of hearts that those feelings are fleeting, you don't really want to hear about some metaphor comparing your life to a beach when in reality, all you want is to *have what you want.*

Like now.

I feel you.

I think one of the hardest places to be is this place called "the meantime."[5] Hard truth, soft pillow? The right relationships, in all areas of life, ultimately happen when the timing is right.

There isn't anything else *to do* in the meantime because, as you know now, people aren't algorithms and human relationships are one particular area of our lives in which action and effort do not beget success or results.

....

5 Iyanla Vanzant wrote an entire book about it.

Frankly, frustratingly, people don't have a hell of a lot of control over it, especially not the timing of it, and it can feel exceptionally challenging, particularly when you're a highly capable, overachieving go-getter who is used to getting shit done and making it happen when you want it.

When you are alone, in any context, and don't want to be, there are moments when *it's just hard*. You choose to cultivate a relationship with yourself, to make it beautiful, and sometimes, in the meantime, it's still fucking hard.

Why? *Because you're human.*

Congratulations on having a normal human experience; trust me, *you are not alone in this.*

I have felt much despair in my own ebbs and flows with the pain of being alone in the context of partnership when what I really desire is to be partnered. When I am doing everything right and still feel that burn of "but what am I supposed to *do* while I'm waiting? How the hell do I survive *in the meantime*?"

If there's nothing to fix, and there's nothing to do, and we have no control over the timeline, how do we honor that?

How can we honor where we're at by holding space for our real life, 3D experience, with all the discomfort and all the frustration of the unknown and all the unrequited expectations of having what we want hand-delivered when we say we're ready?

The answer lies in the question itself, meaning we choose to honor exactly what we're feeling and hold space for ourselves where we're at. The answer is to find a way to bear witness to your own experience of loneliness or longing and to ritualize your sadness and solitude with the sole intention of *ritualizing your sadness in solitude.*

A while ago, I read a book by Jo Piazza called *How to Be Married.* The book is *very* good, as she studies marriage rituals and traditions across the world and writes about them in a playfully nonfiction narrative style.

In one section of the book, Piazza describes going to Mexico, and when looking for an expert in love and union, all the locals tell her to "go see Bobby Klein, go see Bobby Klein." So, she books an appointment with her husband, they go see Bobby Klein, and they have a highly significant experience.

Can you guess what happened next?

I immediately put down the book, did a quick Google search for "Bobby Klein Mexico," and three minutes later, I was booked in to speak with him via Zoom within a week.

Booyah, internet.

I got on the call with him, this LA expat who lives in the hills near Tulum. He had on his white guayabera and round wire-rimmed glasses, wore a long white ponytail, and had an overall peaceful energy. I fully expected him to tell me that yes, I had done everything right, and I could expect love to knock on my door within the next few weeks, two months max.

That was my expectation.

My *reality*? Bobby Klein said that yes, the love I was longing for was very, very real, and . . . I still had a way to go. I immediately broke down crying.

He told me it was as if I had been walking along a bridge, and I'd been walking this *specific* bridge for so long that it felt like I *should be* at the end of it; my ego was telling me I should *definitely* be at the end of it. He told me that while this bridge was long, and I'd done everything right while walking it, I still had a way to go, but that that was a *good* thing, not a bad thing like I was judging it to be.

He said that while I thought I was "here" (at the end), I was actually "here" (I imagined it as the two-thirds mark he pointed to in the air, but who knows); he told me that the walk feels long, and even though I can't see the end and don't know how much longer there is to go, it's going to be *so worth it.*

Partnership—a truly loving union with someone, someone with whom I can raise my family as a team—is the *painfully* simple gift I have been longing for since childhood, the absence of which has been my own personal Achilles' heel and life's greatest pain point.

So, when Bobby Klein didn't give me platitudes of "just keep doing what you're doing" but instead met me in my pain and *taught* me to honor this pain and longing with a ritual, it felt like he was seeing me in my longing and offering me the help I'd been desperately searching for.[6]

He told me to purchase a set of candle holders and white taper candles that I only use for this specific ritual, and he said to start preparing myself mentally and emotionally at night (because he accurately suspected that this pain and longing was greatest at night) after everyone else had gone to bed and the house was quiet and settled. There would be no one on the couch beside me with whom to share the joys, frustrations, or pistachio gelato of the day, and just before the intensity of those feelings came up, I was to light my candles in their beautiful, special candle holders.

That's it: *honor* this pain and longing by *witnessing* my own grief and lighting ritual candles in response.

At first, I was a little bummed that it was that simple.

Sometimes when we're in a lot of emotional pain or turmoil, we want the big, sexy, radically grand and sweeping gestures that really give us the dopamine high of *doing* something.

This honoring ritual was so simple that it almost felt anticlimactic—but I did it anyway.

I went to my favorite little pop-up vintage shop and got five midcentury modern candle holders, then bought our local drugstore out of all the white taper candles they had.

....

6 Sidebar: I kid you not, he also interrupted himself mid-sentence to say, "Oh, I can see that you're going to be teaching this." I was still crying, but I (begrudgingly) took those words to heart, and now, dolly, here we are.

For me, those big feelings of loneliness and monophobia were so real and so intense that I had no idea what to do with them. I could talk to my family, sure. And my therapist. And my coach. And my coach friends. And my journal. And my energy healer. And my tarot reader. And God.

And now, Bobby Klein.

And each of those people and resources were incredibly supportive, consistently.

But still, those feelings of longing and sadness were there, simmering on the back burner like a potpourri you know is there but don't really like the smell of, but it's been going for so long now that you think it's kind of crept into the curtains, and now it's just there, faintly, all the time.

Pervasive.

Emotionally, part of the intensity and part of the pain we feel in this pervasive way comes from *not having a clear plan of how to feel, express, and process what weighs on our hearts and minds*. And so, in addition to the feeling itself, we add layers of judgment, shame, and unrequited expectations that manifest as harsh internal criticism.

What if we had an emergency plan in place to break the proverbial glass when things got really intense? Like the emotional equivalent of "in case of emergency, break glass." You know that hatchet is there if you need it, and all you have to do is break the glass. Now you have a plan, which immediately cuts the anxiety of "yeah, but what do I do if something bad happens?!"

I learned quickly that this ritual element was that emergency plan for my emotional body.

Suddenly I knew "what to do" when those waves of pain or longing started washing over me: I'd comfort myself *beyond* words, *beyond* texting the wrong person at the wrong time—I'd use my action plan of lighting my ritual candles to *witness and honor my grief* in that moment.

That subtle, intentional, and purposeful action allowed me to feel, then channel and redirect the intensity of what I was feeling, in a safe and comfortable way.

Note that this action is not an invitation to bypass, ignore, or repress emotions.

My first book goes into great detail about *how* to feel your feelings, which is an excellent place to start; the ritual element is like the master class for when you are very comfortable in feeling and expressing your emotions yet still feel the need to redirect that emotional energy into something in addition to the *feeling* thereof.

This healing tool has become one of my most valuable ones in my own personal arsenal to help process that energy when it is present, and since I initially adopted it, I've implemented it in other areas of my home life to create an entire ambient space that allows me to *hold space for myself.*

I added new sticks of Palo Santo, candles that smell like California sunset in little amber jars, and incense cones that permeate my house with what I can only imagine John Mayer smells like; I hired a (very cute) electrician to put all my lights on dimmers, bought cocoa powder made of mushrooms to make myself hot cocoa with frothy oat milk at night (without caffeine or an intense sugar crash), and hired a handyman to hang a zigzag string of patio bistro lights across my deck and backyard.

In the warmer months, I dim the lights, burn my candles and incense, leave the door open just enough to get the feeling of fresh air, and make a point of going out to look up at the moon and stars before I go to bed.

It's so slow, so intentional, so calming, and so self-supportive to now have a plan for when these intense feelings come and wash over me. If they are really intense, and especially while I was finessing this ritual to really make it my own, I speak to myself soothingly (my first book has great information on this activity), usually like I am mothering my own inner child and rocking her through her intense sadness, while simply enjoying the process of ritualizing the sadness, which always makes it just a little less sad.

Even though this ritual started as an emergency plan, it has now evolved into something I just do because it *is* so comforting and *feels* so good. And beautifully, after embodying it as a part of my lifestyle?

I feel so much less self-pressure to be partnered than I used to.
I feel so much more at ease, and so much less alone, *in the meantime.*

Not that long ago I was out for a drive and realized I had been feeling something for a while that I was unaccustomed to: *contentment.* Contentment with where exactly I was without the pressure of where I wasn't.

The weight of "being alone" used to feel so intense, so heavy, so pervasive, but now it feels more like "man, this is a long bridge; I better stay hydrated as I keep walking."

Creating that sacred and beautiful ambiance in my living room, the place where I spend most of my time in the evenings, also piqued my curiosity as to "wait . . . if I can create such a pleasure-rich environment that brings such a healing and renewed sense of calm, *where else* can I apply this feeling to my physical environment?"

My (very cute) electrician came back to install more dimmer switches on ALL of the lights in my home so that I could create that same sexy low-light glow in every room. I bought those John Mayer-scented candles and incense cones for my bedroom and added a portable Bluetooth speaker so I could create a super sexy environment in there too. I found a car freshener in the same bougie fragrance from this California candle company I was so into, and I hung it in my car so even my *car* had this sense of atmospheric pleasure.

I added each of these teeny tiny pleasure elements, all stemming from ritualizing sadness and turning it into pleasure, in all physical aspects of my life:

- I bought cozier and more oversized sweaters.
- I bought minimalist gold jewelry that I can wear every day and adorn myself like the goddess I am.
- I bought flowers for our family every week until my cats discovered them and started eating them by the bouquet, then switched to

cutting sprigs of cedar from my yard and placing them in bud vases.

- I got an electronic shiatsu foot massager (and named him Paul) for before-bed foot rubs.
- I placed rolled blankets (and heating pads) in baskets near our couches in the family and living rooms so we can be cozy in an instant.
- I got rid of anything that didn't fit (physically and energetically).
- I hired people to do the things that I am really bad at or just hate doing (like cleaning and writing podcast show notes).
- I took all the energy I wasn't spending on *that* stuff and channeled it into the quality of my work.
- I quit all the shit I'd overcommitted to and stripped down my schedule to what I knew was easy to manage, even as a solo parent of three, and I now say yes *only* to the things that bring me *great* joy.
- I learned to play guitar (not well, but well enough) and came up with my own unexpected covers of pop anthems just because I *liked* singing them.
- I blew up any notions of what business coaches told me *should* work for my business and used these cover songs as cool ways to share my message about mentorship or recent podcast promotion on Instagram.
- I am going for walks more.
- I listened to every episode of every podcast that explored the making of *The Office*.
- I instituted "Burrito Coffee Office" day every Friday morning that kicked off the day with drive-thru burritos and coffee and an episode of *The Office* before I did anything else.

- I looked at my calendar and figured out which months/dates/ seasons felt the hardest being single and strategically booked a weekend away in the woods, months in advance, to create more of those "in case of emergency, break glass" plans that I knew worked so well for me.
- I got very comfortable taking long hot baths. With bubbles. And a book if I want it.
- I use the really good-smelling soap.
- I got a leopard-print bathing cap because man, I hate getting my hair wet, and it makes me feel so fancy.
- I got Belgian linen sheets (worth it) and started sleeping diagonally across my King bed . . . because I *can.*
- I let my hands wander across my body, exploring what felt good to me (not to *perform* pleasure, but to *experience* pleasure) including over the twenty-three-inch scar where my breasts used to be and discovered in this new body what still felt good and mourned the things I couldn't physically feel anymore.
- I found new pleasure practices and accessories that allowed me to feel out the deliciousness of my own divine femininity and sexuality, and I did so on my own terms.
- I became *so present* with my kids.
- I consciously stepped away from my phone and chose to BE with them in whatever way felt right: playing, listening, just being there while they worked away on something.
- I bought a trampoline for them in our yard and sit wrapped in a blanket in the sun on my porch, drinking coffee, watching them bounce. My youngest even commented once how nice it was to just BE there together, doing different things beside each other.

- I read. I nap. I watch *Magic Mike.*
- I pee outside in the dark if I want to.

I.
Tapped.
Into.
Pleasure.

And before I knew it, tapping into pleasure didn't even require conscious thought anymore. I naturally just started doing the things that felt *really fucking great*. I infused more intention behind almost all things I did, so that even watering the garden, which ordinarily I hate, felt pleasurable because I found this cool black hose with a gold spout that—wait for it—matches my design aesthetic.

This was next-level care of self by employing Emotional Alchemy all over my life, simply by choosing *the ritual of making things beautiful.*

I felt like I was the living embodiment of the Elsie de Wolf quote: "I am going to make everything around me beautiful—that will be my life." It was like I had found a way to ritualize and then alchemize those pervasive feelings of longing into a new way of living my life, exactly as it is, and being able to enjoy it by just *letting it be what it is.*

Less *do*ing, more *be*ing.

Later I had the chance to interview celebrity psychotherapist and author of *Boundary Boss*, Terri Cole, on my podcast, chatting about how to end codependency. When she told me in detail that next-level self-care was *the* antidote to codependent patterns, I think I laughed out loud and started recounting each of those little measures I'd consciously taken in my own life to make it richer in pleasure, and she assured me that this indeed was *exactly* what was required to put an end to those old toxic patterns.

Because when you are taking care of yourself—hands on, authentically attentive, genuine care of your Self—there isn't room to fear how you may or may not be letting someone else down or to worry about pleasing someone else in order to get your own needs met.

You just . . . *meet your own needs.*

Self-care is highly misappropriated to sell you shit you don't need (facial toner and masques, I'm looking at *you*), but really, self-care just means "taking care of your Self, taking care of your *soul.*"

There's the reframe:
What if you could shift self-care into *soul care*?
What would feel good for your *soul*?
What do *you* need? How do *you* get those needs met? What would feel really fucking great for *you*?

Poet Mark Anthony once said that loving someone is like lighting a fire in their heart and attending to it for life.

In our efforts to self soothe our sadness or other heavy feelings by ritualizing them, that's exactly what you're doing: *You are attending to the fire in your own heart for life.* It creates an atmosphere of deep peace. And creating that atmosphere of deep peace in your external environment with the sole intention of ritualizing your sadness in solitude brings an even deeper sense of peace internally while creating the feeling that you belong to yourself.

And when you belong to yourself, the truth and beauty of it is that you are never really alone.

CHAPTER EIGHTEEN

RECLAIM YOUR JOY

"If only I had a boyfriend," I thought to myself.

It was fresh off the heels of divorce, selling what had been our family home, and it felt like the early stages of the dust of change starting to settle. My girlies were with their dad for the weekend, and it was a spectacular day in early summer, but I was alone in our sweet little rented cottage-style home . . . feeling particularly sorry for myself.

"If only I had a boyfriend," I thought. "Then I'd have something to do this weekend, and I could actually have some fun." Out of nowhere, that little voice popped up and confronted me on what I was thinking.

"Then what?" it asked.

"Pardon?" I replied, baffled. I was still not used to or even fully comfortable with what was also the early stages of a spiritual awakening.

"Then what?" I heard again. *"If only you had a boyfriend . . . then what? What would you do?"*

"Uh, we'd . . . go for a drive."
"Okay. Where?"

"We'd . . . drive out to The County. For brunch. And we'd sit at the bar, enjoying coffee and Indie music while we waited for our Eggs Benny."
"Okay. And?"

"We'd . . . look out at the lake, meander around, and poke into all those cute shops I've seen on the country roads."
"Okay. And?"

"We'd . . . stop for coffee again at any place we found that looked cool. Ooh! And at a farm stand, just because we could, and because it's raspberry season."
"Okay. And?"

"That's it. That would be a perfect day we'd spend together, just driving, drinking coffee, exploring, listening to music, all with no agenda."
"Okay. And what would you wear?"

"Um, I'd wear those sexy ripped jean shorts with that white button-down. Wavy hair. Blowing in the breeze. Dark sunnies. Red lips."

"Get dressed. Go do that."

This was a moment.

It was the first moment, being freshly single after a fourteen-year relationship and in the thick of much codependency and people pleasing, that it occurred to me that *I could do whatever I wanted.* I could do *whatever felt good to me,* and there'd be no one there to judge, critique, or tell me why we couldn't go. There was no one postponing, naysaying, or suggesting anything other than what I thought would be a perfect day.

It was the first moment that it occurred to me that I could have all of it, *without relying on anyone else to give me permission* to do it: my fun, my pleasure, my experience, my *joy* was dependent only on my own imagination, and I could give myself permission to do it all.

So, I did all those things, right down to the farm stand for raspberries.
It was *amazing.*
It was *freedom.*
It was the beginning of *a lot* of adventures and solo travel.

I realized very quickly that all my previous adventures and travels had been shared with the person with whom I'd been in a *fourteen-year* relationship, meaning that every time I had a travel or adventure memory, it was tarnished in some way by remembering the pain (or the joy, then the loss of that joy) from my past.

My partner of fourteen years and I got together when I was twenty-one, and I hadn't really done anything *on my own* yet; the painfully challenging aspect was that all those adventure memories felt like they were a part of a shared history, a history whose context had changed so dramatically that it no longer felt like my own, which then felt like I had no safe memories of adventure or joy to claim as my own.

I *immediately* set to work creating opportunities for my own passion, adventure, and exploration. I wanted to reclaim my joy.

I decided to drive to Detroit. I'd always wanted to go and just hadn't had the chance. I talked to a friend who loved the city and knew it well and who basically gave me an itinerary of cool highlights to go and check out, from bakeries to markets to restaurants and galleries.

Off I went. I hopped in my station wagon and drove the six-hour trip. I went to the Eastern Market and sang karaoke, sober, in the daytime with people cheering me on as they passed by. Afterward, I listened to *actual* Motown singers get up and do almost a full set, while we all cheered them on, only to walk their purple-suited and wing-tipped-shoed selves *back to their Cadillac.*

I stood in the open-air market, eating, drinking, hanging out, and laughing with people I'd never see again but who felt like new friends.

I went to cool cafés for my first pour-over coffee, saw an American photography exhibit at the Detroit Institute of the Arts, and stood in total wonder during the audio–visual tour of Diego Rivera's *Detroit Industry Murals.* I drove around, taking my own photos of all the street art. I met a friend from Michigan who drove down to join me for dinner and drinks.

I went to a dive bar specifically to hear the house band of twenty years, and I hung out with a group of American couples that were visiting from Indiana or somewhere. I then went for a Coney Island hot dog at 2:00 a.m. and bought a bunch of those paper hats they wear to bring back as souvenirs.

I capped it all off by meeting up with another couple of friends in the park for the gospel Sunday morning of the Detroit Jazz Festival. It was a perfect weekend, based on what felt good and what would bring me joy, and as I was focused on bringing that level of joy and adventure into my life, I was building up a new bank of memories that were *sacredly my own.*

On another weekend, after seeing an ad online, I drove to Elkhorn, Wisconsin, to the Instagram-famous "Camp Wandawega," for a creative entrepreneur retreat, where I met one of my closest friends for the first time, solo paddled the lake at sunrise, and hooked up with the maintenance guy (twice)—drinking whiskey by the fire and making out in the Airstream.

Joy.

I drove with my friend Amy to New York City in a car that Cadillac Canada gifted me for the weekend, with the express purpose of seeing the opening exhibit of one of my favorite Scandinavian artists, Christiane Spangsberg, at a gallery in the Lower East Side. Intent on buying one of her pieces, I got there just in time to have my hand on my credit card to purchase the last remaining piece (and the one I'd had my heart set on) when someone *phoned in* their order one minute before I could complete the transaction.

I looked at Amy and almost *died* laughing, as we simultaneously processed the fact that we could have just *skipped the eight-hour drive through New Jersey rush hour* and *phoned* in an order. It was priceless. Then we sipped rosé on a Lower East Side patio with a couple of Jewish finance guys, stayed in Brooklyn the rest of the weekend, and managed to get a reservation at the bar for a one Michelin star Mexican restaurant in Queens.

Joy.

I drove to New Hampshire.
Chicago.
All the way from LA to Seattle up the coast of Highway 1.
I made decisions based on the simple metric of what felt good, and it changed my life. In those moments of cultivating freedom and memories, I was cultivating a keen sense of *who I was* as a woman.

I reclaimed my joy.

One of my go-to questions in my coaching and mentorship practice is to ask my client, "What brings you joy?" I cannot tell you how often that question is met with a long pause, silence, then tears, followed by "Oh my God, *I have no idea.*"

How many of us are taught or learn vicariously from a young age that our needs don't matter? That we're an inconvenience? That there's work to be done? That indulgence shouldn't be indulged? That whatever someone else wants to do is what *you* should want to do, and that to compromise or acquiesce in the spirit of selflessness and taking care of others is a *revered* quality, even when it's something you *really* don't want to do?

Cut to the feeling so many of us have that in our selflessness, we are literally *without self.*

We feel like we just don't belong, whether that's in our social groups, community, work culture, or (ouch) even in our families. Is that any surprise, though, when you look at it through the lens that very few of us are encouraged from an early age to just do what feels good instead of doing what feels good for someone else?

Sometimes we feel like we don't belong because we don't even know what would make us feel happy or joyful enough to *want* to belong. How can we belong to or feel like we are a part of a group when we don't even belong to or feel like we are a part of *ourselves*?

And so begins the work of truly learning yourself.
How?

Long story short? You flash back to when you were a kid, before anyone told you who you were, and tap into what made you feel instantly free, happy, at ease, and joyful, and you do *that.*

Short story long? The problem is that for some people, even tapping into *that* is quite challenging, especially if trauma was present. They don't remember, or possibly didn't ever experience, a time in which it was safe or available to *be* free, happy, at ease, and joyful. That sense of not truly belonging and disconnect may have started very early.

If that is the case, and this exercise feels challenging, you can start simply by asking, "What would YOU like to do?"

So many of my own overwhelming feelings of not belonging and not being chosen were informed by family narratives from my childhood; I felt so separate from and out of synch with my immediate family that I *vividly* remember swimming in our backyard and ducking under for long periods of time, without anyone seeing, to *cry out* my frustrations of feeling like I just didn't belong.

And I watched as that feeling of disconnection and simultaneous fear of not belonging spilled over into my friendships, marriage, relationships, and jobs. I did whatever it took to feel chosen and included because I felt—for decades—that I didn't belong *anywhere*. To *anyone*.

For a long time I felt like an outsider, and I would overcompensate through my own listing and toxic behavioral patterns of fawning and people pleasing until I began the deep and *multiyear* process of the inner work that would ultimately lead me home to belong to myself.

I remember hearing that pivotal Maya Angelou quote, the one that opens this book, on one of my solo road trips to the US, and it hit me like the hardest truth with the *softest* pillow of all:

"You only are free when you realize you belong no place—you belong every place—no place at all. The price is high. The reward is great."

Whoa.

Was I not, in fact, the only person to ever feel like I didn't belong? Was this struggle, this longing, this unrequited need to feel whole just a part of the human experience?

It was revolutionary: *I was not alone in my experience of feeling so alone.*

It dawned on me that what if, in addition to not really knowing or loving or even understanding who we are for many years or even decades, it is just *a part of the human condition* to feel like an outsider?

What if it is just a part of our own self-creation, walking down that long path of life that makes us *feel* like we don't belong only to bring us to the existential understanding and realization that you always belong to yourself?

If "belonging" isn't conditional upon the circumstances or acceptance of others—it's a choice you make to commit to belonging to yourself, making your Self your one true home—it becomes a lot easier to reframe every other connection you make along that walk home *a part of* your experience, not *the point of* your experience.

As we're sorting through the layers of someone else's expectations, challenging false narratives about who we are and what we like, and unlearning patterns of people pleasing and codependency (almost always developed as self-protection measures to keep us emotionally safe), we are unlearning our false self and (re)learning our *true* self.

This next-level commitment allows us to walk our path with sincere, not performative, authenticity and have a purpose-driven life of genuine connection.

You better believe *the price is high.*
And you better believe *the reward is great.*

It's not sexy.
It's not a peak experience that gives you a quick hit of dopamine.
It's not for the faint of heart.

It *can* feel lonely, and it *can* feel isolating en route to truly, as Plato said, *know[ing] thyself.* The reward is the feeling of being at home wherever you go, because wherever you go, there you are.

The alternative is also to feel lonely or to feel isolated but to be surrounded in less-than-genuine connection while you feel that way.

Ultimately, it's your decision to choose your kind of lonely: the kind of lonely that comes from surface-level connections within real substance or the kind of lonely that comes from a focused commitment to honoring every part of you that makes you, *you.*

For me, my kind involves road trips. Tacos. Making life beautiful. Playing guitar and singing along at the top of my lungs. Dancing in the kitchen, even when no one is around. Being in the woods near water. Fine-line tattoos. Acting out weird and funny voices at the dinner table with my kids. Pizza on Fridays. Coffee on the deck. Laughing as a hobby.

That's what makes me feel like me. *What makes you feel like you?* What lights you up purely by *feeling free to be who you are?*

In any new relationship, there is a learning curve in which you just can't wait to devour each and every fact you don't yet know about the person; you're catching up on learning who they are and what they've done and what they love and what they've yet to do—everything you missed along the way of not knowing them until that moment.

What if you turned that learning experience inward? What if you played catch-up with getting to know yourself and learned all the things you've been longing for without ever having permission to acknowledge that longing along the way?

What if you reframed this season of your life to taking the time you're walking along your path—especially if it has felt like you've been walking it alone with no significant other's path converging on, or anywhere near, yours—and treat the *getting to know you* process like getting to know the ultimate lover of your life. Figure out who *you* are and what you're about.

This time is *precious*: It's the freedom to reclaim your joy and fall in love with yourself, establishing the strongest foundation upon which you can build many other relationships (in your work, life, and love) as time goes on.

When you feel safe to experience that intimate connection of being in love with who you are, as you are, *that* is when you feel like you belong to yourself.

And when you belong to yourself, the truth and beauty of it is that you are never really alone.

CHAPTER NINETEEN

LOST AND FOUND

I have no sense of geographical direction. None. I rely heavily on GPS and Google Maps to get me where I'm going until I've been somewhere so often that I can start to landmark it. Ish.

So, years ago, when I decided to live my dream trip, I rented a brand-new Mustang convertible and drove the Pacific Coast Highway (PCH) all the way from Los Angeles to Seattle. Because of my, uh, *issues* with geographical direction, it shouldn't have come as a major surprise to me when I inevitably got lost . . . but it did.

The point of this epic road trip was to:
1. Stop dreaming about this trip and do it.
2. Forgive myself for a lot of past mistakes.
3. Stop for tacos along the way.

That's it. I'd been at a conference in LA, I had a cousin working at Amazon who lived in Seattle, and I needed to be back home in time for Mother's Day. I had a start point, an end point, a siiiiick car, and a tight timeframe. Like, seventy-two-hours tight.

Now, for context, driving the coastline through California up to Washington through Oregon is at least a 1,500-mile trip; that's about twenty-four hours of solid driving. I thought that driving the PCH would be like it is in Malibu (what you see in all the movies): an expansive, multilane road, nice and flat and open, with the ocean at your side.

Turns out the PCH is this way for maybe 100 miles *total*. One-fifteenth of the trip is easy—and I think that's being generous. The rest is *very* challenging.

I was so focused on making this trip happen that it is possible I *may* have neglected to appreciate the intensity of a 1,500-mile drive, in three days, as a solo driver. It's also possible that I *may* have neglected to appreciate that the part of the trip that takes you through the California Redwood Forest is, in many places, almost a *sheer vertical* with zero guardrails and several logging trucks, meaning that if you slip off the road, veering to avoid one of those many logging trucks that seem to drive only in the middle of an already narrow road, you're fucked.

All I knew is that I needed to realize my dream.
Knowing my timeline was tight, I had three road trip goals:
1. See McWay Falls and Cove in Big Sur, California.
2. Have coffee in Portland.
3. Eat all the tacos, everywhere.

So, I set off, driving through the actual Hollywood Hills, saw "Debbie" from *Shameless* hiking with her friends near the iconic Hollywood sign, and made my way north. I drove past Malibu and headed into Ventura (through which I teed up "Ventura" by Lucinda Williams on my playlist), hell-bent on finding this waterfall, loving my life.

When my GPS tried to take me off the main road, away from the ocean, and knowing that the ocean view was why this drive would be so special, I decided to "wing it" and figure out how to get back to the PCH, navigating to the falls on my own.

I mean, how hard could it be? I'd just use the ocean as my landmark . . .

I pieced together where the falls were and where I thought I'd need to be to get there on my way to Seattle, and I was feeling good. "I'm doing it. I'm living it. Hell, I don't even need a map; I'm just one sexy badass woman, driving this sexy badass car, out on the open road, feeling the ocean breeze in my hair."

And that's when I realized something: The ocean was on the wrong side of me; my geography may not be good, but it's good enough to know that while driving north on the west coast, the ocean *should* be on the left. It wasn't.

It felt like my entire stomach dropped out.

Somehow, I'd gotten myself turned around without noticing, and instead of travelling north for the past two to three hours, I'd been going *south*, made worse by the Friday afternoon rush hour that was literally backed up to a standstill . . . for hours.

Doing some quick mental math, I realized the timing of this directional gaffe took *a solid ten hours* off my trip. The falls, literally the only land-mark I wanted to see, would not be an option anymore if I wanted to finish the trip, drop off the car as arranged, see my cousin, *and* get back home to my family in time.

It sucked.

But, having to make accommodations for this mistake, I did end up having *lots* of time to drive through and explore the redwood forest, as perilously white-knuckling of a drive as it was, and I actually got to drive *through* one of the trees that was wide enough for my Mustang to fit. It was so cool.

- I stopped in Carmel by the Sea.
- Took in the view with coffee at Mendocino.
- Had dinner at this retro pizza place called Pinky's (full of old-school arcade games and super-hot dads) in Petaluma and played pinball while I waited for my slice.
- Found a room at an inn in the middle of the night and joined the staff for champagne at the bar. (They weren't really open, they just kind of felt sorry for me.)
- Drove through wine country at sunrise, in the mist, with the roof open, listening to "Magnolia" by J.J. Cale.

- Cried out loud years—*years*—of self-forgiveness with the wind whipping at my hair.
- Had coffee in Portland at an ultracool café, after spending as few hours of the night as possible in a room that rivalled the Bates Motel.
- Spent a day exploring Seattle with my cousin.
- Ate tacos all the way up the coast.

It was perfect, and although I got *lost* in diverting from the original vision of what I'd planned, I *found* so many more memories in the meantime.

Because sometimes you really do need to get lost in order to get found. And as needle-point-cushion-y as it sounds, the journey really *is* the destination.

Having been single (and physically alone) for what felt like an eternity was absolutely *not what I had planned*; it was absolutely not a part of the vision. And as you have read, it caused so much pain and worry and anxiety along the way: I have had to adapt and readapt over and over while being able to find the courage and resolve to remain hopeful about realizing, and even feeling *safe to have*, my vision.

About three weeks before my fortieth birthday, I was driving along a back road near the woods when it hit me:
I was really happy.

Like, *really* happy. And it wasn't that dopamine-high,

fresh-off-an-adventure, or new-Tinder-match kind of happy—I was just in this calm state of contentment that didn't *come from* anything, it just *was*.

I wasn't *do*ing, I was *be*ing.

And I was thinking that I was just so happy there on my own: It didn't come from anything, it didn't come from anyone, it just felt like I'd learned to consistently figure out how to get my needs met to the point where I didn't even have to think about it anymore. I just *met* them, and it felt really good.

And that's when it hit me like a hard truth, soft pillow that I would not, COULD not have reached this state of inner calm had I not had *all* this time on my own.

Oof.

For so long I craved that feeling of calm born from a deep feeling of safety and security, and I assumed that would come from being in a partnered, committed relationship with, say, a 6'4" former athlete from Texas who drives a vintage truck and has made a new life for himself by retiring in Toronto, where we'd meet, and he'd split his time between the city and the country with me and my girls.

Or, you know, John Krasinski.

Had I met this guy, the one I thought would bring me that deep sense of comfort, calm, and security (while cooking family dinner, dancing me around the kitchen, playing guitar, and building a treehouse for the kids), I wouldn't have had the chance to cultivate these feelings of comfort, calm, and security *within* myself.

Which brings me back to the point of this chapter: that the journey itself *is* the destination.

Getting lost feels *so awful* while you're in it because while you're in it, you can't see what you're gaining—you only see what you *lack*. You can't see that you're never really lost at all, you're just taking a different route to the same end goal that looks a little (and yes, sometimes a lot) different than you initially thought.

Contentment, happiness, joy . . . they don't "come" from somewhere, they are created by you from within. Just like memories are not created by setting out to make a memory, they're created by the crazy stuff that happens while we're living out our intentions, and beyond.

Clarify the feeling, hold the vision, trust the process.

I bet you know how easy it is to chase the feeling of happiness that comes from somewhere else, like chasing a peak experience and the high that comes with it. You know you're in that chasing external and impermanent happiness when you're stuck not in the pursuit of happiness, but in the *happiness of pursuit*, and you need to chase things just for the high the chasing gives you.

True joy, true contentment, and true happiness come from the inner peace and calm *you create* by living the life and making the decisions that feel right for you. Every time it feels like you're lost and alone, you're really just finding out more about who you really are.

And the more you find out about who you are, the more you belong to yourself.

And when you belong to yourself, the truth and beauty of it is that you are never really alone.

CHAPTER TWENTY

THE GUEST BOOK

My dad built me a treehouse and a tiny cabin in our backyard when I was a little girl, and I never really got over how awesome that was.

I can still see this image I have of my dad's giant 6'3" frame wearing a surgical skullcap I assume he "borrowed" from his work at the hospital, striding across the lawn with a bundle of two-by-fours under his arm, whistling The Stones' "Beast of Burden," having an overall air of happiness, ease, and levity.

The treehouse had a staircase going up, a slide coming down, and a straight, vertical ladder ascending to the tiny Crow's Nest he built as a lookout in the oak tree. It was amazing.

The tiny cabin he built right afterward we called the Playhouse. It had a lofted area, where I think he may have kept some of his tools, and an eighties-style wooden play kitchen for me. I remember picking little bouquets of forget-me-nots growing on either side of the step that led to the front door of the Playhouse as he worked away in the yard.

As a tween and then teen, I LOVED sleeping up in the treehouse by myself or with a friend, bringing licorice and our purple sleeping bags out there, setting up camp to spy on my neighbors and any passersby, stakeout style. We never saw anything particularly interesting, living in a quiet residential area of an upper middle-class neighborhood in a small town, but still. The thrill of what we *might* see while completely hidden away was worth the high of anticipation. And in the morning, we'd gather up our stuff and slide down to start the day.

Even as an adult, I have this memory ingrained into the fabric of who I am because renting unique and sometimes off the grid treehouses, tiny houses, and cabins is one of my all-time favorite hobbies.[7]

Going on a road trip (often solo) into the woods and exploring a new place that someone has built with their own hands . . . and just *be*ing in the solitude of it all is just the right amount of adventure for me.

Something I've noticed in almost every cool cabin I've been to is that they all have (an 11:00 a.m. checkout and) a guest book. And as someone

....

7 I actually wrote this specific chapter in the loft bed of an off-grid treehouse in Muskoka, Ontario, and I edited in the tiny A-frame cabin on the same property. I even brought licorice and my purple sleeping bag with me.

who usually does these trips alone, and who usually gets bored a bit faster than expected until I can allow myself the recalibration of being away from screens and societal demands, I often read the guest books, which are often quite well penned.

And it always reminds me of this universal human truth: We have a need to be known.

We need to know that we are known.
We need to know that we are seen.
We need to know that our experience is being witnessed and that our existence matters.

And so, we sign the guest book to write an account that *we were here.*

It got me thinking. What is the "guest book" of our lives?

If life is a solo journey, and the journey itself is the destination, how do we make our mark on the world and ensure that our tree makes a sound when it falls in the forest, even if no one else is around to hear it? How do we leave behind the guest book of our lives and let it be known that we were known?

The simplest, shortest answer?

We focus on the feeling we want, and we work to create that feeling now.
We ask ourselves, "What would feel good?" and then give ourselves permission to DO that.

We slow down the pace and allow ourselves to be present in whatever it is we're doing, one moment at a time.

That's it: It really is that simple; it really is that complicated.
And sometimes it is that anticlimactic: We just kinda BE.

It can feel frustrating when we're walking along our path, figuring it out as we go. It can feel equally frustrating when we think our path is going one way and it suddenly takes a sharp turn in a different or even opposite direction from where we think we're "supposed" to go.

That doesn't mean our path is wrong.
That doesn't mean we were wrong for thinking, or even wanting, a different direction.

It just means we're walking our unique path, in alignment with the plan, exactly as we're "supposed" to.

The pages of our "guest book" become filled with stories of who we've met, what we've done, feelings we've had, signs from God that this could serve us well, signs from God that we were getting close to something that *wouldn't* have served us at all. Our guest book becomes an account of who we are and who we've been along the way, marked with memories and synchronicities designed for our specific purpose in this lifetime.

Yes, it's nice when someone else reads our guest book; it can feel like validation that the experience we're having is real, significant. Other times it can feel slightly disappointing when someone else reads our guest book, like trying to capture a photograph of the most beautiful sunset or rainbow you've ever seen: Sure, the photo looks good, but man, you should have seen it *in person*.

When we can shift our focus away from someone else bearing witness to our experience to simply *living* our experience, we also shift our perspective and expectations of what we're really experiencing. Honoré de Balzac said that "solitude is fine, but you need to tell someone that solitude is fine," which is the nineteenth-century equivalent of making an Instagram post telling people you're going offline for a while.

We want someone to witness our experience.
We need to know that our experience is being witnessed.

What if we became aware of and embodied the fact that we could bear powerful witness to *our own* experience and that sharing that account with someone else is a delicious bonus? Having someone witness your truth is *so empowering*, and still, what if, even in the meantime, it could become enough to witness it for ourselves? What if it could become enough to reclaim our joy for ourselves because it felt good versus chasing the feeling of "feeling good" coming from sharing the joy with someone else?

It's a huge ask, I know.

And if we can get comfortable with the enough-ness of claiming our experience as our own, we are actually empowering ourselves to be enough as the witness. Seeing ourselves as both the do-er and the watch-er allows us to dwell in the space of both/and, understanding that we alone are enough.

Which creates the ultimate sense of belonging because it empowers you to belong to yourself.

And when you belong to yourself, the truth and beauty of it is that you are never really alone.

CHAPTER TWENTY-ONE

CHOSEN

I remember looking at my calendar one day in August, eyes creeping ahead to November, the month that would mark the fifth anniversary of calling time of death on my first marriage and lighting the life *I knew* on fire to have the life that *I know* rise up from the ashes.

It was heavy.

Five years brought a lot of things my way, including *a lot* of adversity through which I found *a lot* of triumph. But the one triumph it did not bring, in case I haven't mentioned it enough in the first 200 or so pages of this book, was the arrival of the man of my dreams.

Which was heavy too.

I remember sitting in quiet self-reflection and taking stock of my life—what it had looked like, what I thought it would look like, what it actually looked like, and I felt an intense sadness wash over me. Knowing that our feelings are feedback that give us incredibly valuable insights as to what still needs to be healed, I started to explore what this feeling was called and what it was telling me in order to get a sense of what needed some attention, care, and healing.

The sadness came from the story I was telling myself: "Nobody ever chooses me . . . therefore, I will *never* be chosen." When I asked myself, "Is that story true?" I realized—gulp—fuck.

Yes, it was.

As I explored in my first book:
My mom didn't *choose* me when she left our family early on.
My stepmom didn't *choose* me when she engaged in decades of emotional abuse.
My dad didn't *choose* me when he buried himself in work, pretending it was all okay.
My friends didn't *choose* me when I went through divorce.
My many crushes, flings, and almost relationships didn't *choose* me, even after I'd given it my all to be seen and known. Even after I had done so many years of the work, expecting a magical cookie in the shape of Mr. Wonderful waiting for me at some imaginary and self-imposed deadline I called "turning forty."

It got heavier.

I sat there for a minute feeling *very sad,* like—wow. This story hurts so much because it's *so* true, and I have several examples consciously proving it to be true.

And as I sat there feeling very low and even ashamed of this narrative that felt uncomfortably embodied, I had one of those beautiful, quiet, subtle, yet indelibly impactful spiritual download moments:

I chose me.

In every relationship, every relational dynamic, and every emotional trauma I *could* have:

- Turned to drugs, disordered eating, lots of risky sex, or other self-harming behaviors to numb the pain of being unloved by my parents—so that I wouldn't be alone.
- Stayed in a dead marriage that made me feel like I was drowning on the inside—so that I wouldn't be alone.
- Maintained the illusion of friendship with people I knew didn't care about me—so that I wouldn't be alone.
- Foregone the aggressive and curative cancer treatments for the sake of how I'd look—so that I wouldn't feel the fear of being alone (while also being flat and bald).

I *could* have given up.
But I didn't.

And if you're reading this, I can assure you: *neither did you.*

At every moment, every painful moment, I consistently chose to do what felt right for me. It didn't necessarily feel good, and it sure as hell didn't feel easy; it felt *right.*

And in doing the right thing for me, consistently protecting my mental, emotional, and physical health and energies, oh my gawwwwwd, I was choosing *me.*

That moment of awareness almost took the wind out of me. It felt like "that scene" in *The Usual Suspects* when they start to piece it all together that Kevin Spacey was Keyser Söze all along, suddenly seeing the clues that had been in front of their faces the whole damn time.

I.
Fucking.
Chose.
Me.

In sickness and health, for richer and for poorer, for better and for worse, I. Chose. Me.
I chose to *be there* for me. To *show up for* me. To *support* me, and to *ask for help supporting me* when I just couldn't do it alone.

Having that deep realization of self-trust, self-love, and self-acceptance made me take pause and get out of my own head. It made me get out of my own story and start to flip the script on the "yeah but nobody ever chooses meeeee" narrative.

I realized, too, right then and there, that if I chose me, then *somebody already chose me.*

And if I already chose me, then *I was always with me.*

And if I had been able to find the inner strength and resolve it took to always choose and be with me (even in the seasons during which I *really* wanted to give up and self-abandon), then there must be something unseen and bigger than me guiding and supporting me to do so.

If I was always with me, and if I was always with something unseen and bigger than me . . .

Damn.

That means I was never, *ever* alone.
And neither were you.
Ever.
It was just a part of the plan.

This discovery felt amazing and free until I looked down at the fourth finger of my left hand and found it to be almost painfully bare, save for the well-manicured nail on the tip. I heard this very fearful and insidious, egoic voice pop up to tell me, *"Nice try; if you were really chosen, there would be a ring on that finger right now."*

And almost instantly I knew what to do: put a ring on that finger right now.

Weddings and commitment ceremonies are all about honoring the divine union between two people in celebration of their love and trust of one another, honored with ritual, ceremony, beauty, and fun, then symbolizing it with a ring on the finger.

Discovering the divine union of the relationship I had chosen to have with myself felt like something worthy of celebrating my self-love and self-trust and honoring it with ritual, ceremony, beauty, and fun, then symbolizing it with a ring on the left ring finger.

So, I consulted the "Forest Elopement" Pinterest board I'd started years ago and started putting it into action:

- I booked a weekend, on my five-year "divorce-aversary," at a cabin in the woods up north and invited my friend Nina, who's a hella talented photographer, to come along.
- I purchased a little white cotton shift dress to pair with a vintage fur stole.
- I commissioned a bespoke flower crown and hand-tied bouquet in tones of burgundy, blush, and evergreen from my florist friend.
- I planned a boho-inspired "aisle" in the woods with a macrame hanging and a beautiful Kilim-style runner I bought at a Brooklyn flea market, and I planned which song I wanted playing as I walked down it.
- I wrote a simple and beautiful vow to myself to read into the mirror I'd place at the end of the aisle . . .
- . . . and I bought a minimalist thin gold band, then had it engraved with a little love note inside.

And after the ceremony, we went for tacos.

It was so beautiful.
It felt so special and intentional to mark what had had the capacity to be such a painful moment of my life and make it purposefully my own. Emotional Alchemy at its finest.

This whole experience really got me thinking:
If you can't clap with one hand, maybe it's time to consider making a different kind of music.

No matter how much we try ("we" meaning all recovering perfectionists and people pleasers here), *we just cannot control all the circumstances of our lives.*

In fact, the only thing we ever really have control over is how we respond and react to the circumstances of our lives. And when we wrap our heads around that hard truth, soft pillow, we find ourselves in a much more empowered position with true agency over our own emotional experience and regulation.

There's an over-memed and misappropriated Law of Attraction concept that if we want something badly enough, think about it long enough, work for it hard enough, we can have whatever we want. At first blush, that seems empowering: you'll no longer be a victim to your life. You'll take charge and take the reins to get what you want.

Cool.

But that's about 10 percent true.

The other 90 percent that hardly anyone talks about with any degree of competency or depth is that we can have a vision for our lives, and we can invest all the right time and energy to support that vision, and we may still not have any control of the timing or of the fact that it is all bigger than us and that what we want specifically may come to us in a different way.

We don't want the thing; we want the feeling we think the thing is going to give us.
And that subtle nuance has a lot of ripple effects on our lives and expectations thereof.

The Buddhists say that "life is suffering," and our peace and happiness comes from figuring out how to be present in the moment, cope with, and learn from the suffering. For me, that will always be found in answering, "How can I make this beautiful? How can I use Emotional Alchemy to turn this suffering into something uniquely my own?"

What does it mean for you? Knowing that the dream of having an endlessly smooth-sailing life of happiness and luxury is an illusion, commodified into something (many, many somethings) to be bought and sold), how do you get clear on your own loving and healthy strategy to cope with the ebb and flow?

This clarity is what my own professional practice centers on. It's why I write books on how to specifically *choose* to do that, and it's what I teach people to do in my private mentorship. We figure out what that vision is and what that feeling is you long to have. How do we create both while navigating the unseen parts of the plan that pop up?

Again, we never really want the thing, we want the feeling we think the thing is going to give us. So, when we focus on what the *feeling* is that we want to cultivate, it better expands and informs our true vision coming into our reality.

The other zinger is that when you think back to the phenomenal power of our subconscious mind and how it really is our built-in internal personal security team designed to look for and keep us safe from any and all kinds of danger, *sometimes it doesn't feel too safe to want what we want,* so we self-sabotage in order to keep what we *know* to be true, to *be* true.

Because again, if that is what has been established as our neurological and emotional baseline of "what feels safe," we unconsciously work to preserve that safety.

Wanting something, thinking about something, and working hard for something will never be enough—repeat, *never* be enough—if the something that you want and/or think about and work hard for conflicts with your subconscious beliefs and thus your internal feelings of neurological safety.

Isn't that wild?

When we ignore the 90 percent—the place where *literally all* the subconscious awareness and unlearning happens—we trap ourselves in a place of lack and of never actually receiving what it is we want in the first place, including the *feeling* of what that is.

Now, I'm not saying that we can't have what we want. I am a *huge* believer that we want what we want for a reason and that that reason is likely a part of our Soul's overall plan for us in this lifetime.

So, while I may have that whisper of "the understated, confident, out-doorsy, wealthy, burly (and well-hung) man who is loving, kind, down to earth, emotionally intelligent, ready to be a husband and stepdad and who comes from a big family, makes me laugh my head off and can build tree forts and gingerbread houses with my kids . . . or John Krasinski" as what my heart and soul deeply desire, *you* may have the whisper to:

- Travel all seven continents.
- Take surf school in Hawaii.
- Build generational wealth doing what you love in a way that was previously unavailable to the generations of women who came before you.
- Quietly weed your garden in the country after waking up to spectacular sex and coffee.
- Wear the Prada shift dress to a night of glamorous cocktails with the who's who of the music industry.
- Leave the seven-figure salary and open a small private practice that buys you more time with your kids.
- Open a rotisserie chicken stand on the beach.
- Just. Feel. Free.

We each have a dream.

While many in the coaching/self-development industry advocate that "if your dreams don't scare you, they're not big enough," you know I call shade on that in favor of embodying the divine wisdom that your dream is *your* dream; it may be juicy and enormous, but it may also be so beautifully quiet and *simple* it scares you.

The size and scope of the dream is inconsequential; the only thing that matters is that you trust that your dream, your vision, and your *deep desire* is there for a reason—and that alone makes it worthy of pursuit.

It's your plan.

What does this plan have to do with being alone?

Everything. Because that dream is yours alone to have and yours alone to pursue.

When you shift your thinking to:
- being in deep belief that you want what you want for a reason
- following all the little cosmic breadcrumbs your intuition offers you
- looking for 'expanders:' conscious proof showing you that *what you want exists* in real life
- taking action on healing wounds and overcoming obstacles that pop up to obstruct that dream from being yours . . .

. . . it also shifts your intention behind making your dream your reality.

Suddenly you're not focused on "getting what you want when you want it," *you're cultivating the co-creation of your soul's true plan* and getting comfortable in being curious about the process of what happens next:

"How can I use this experience as a steppingstone to bringing me home to my Self?"

It brings you into alignment with the abundance that *the journey itself is the destination.*

And that is a motherfucker of a solitary process.

As you know, there are parts of that path you walk with others, and still, even when you're completely in stride, the path you're walking is your own.

When you start to normalize the process of learning to be in partnership with yourself, you prioritize the imperative value of knowing yourself, loving yourself, and enjoying spending time with yourself and doing so in a way that feels really good for you.

That's the easy part.
The hard part is *embodying* that process while processing the liminal space between what is and what is yet to be.

My friend Shani Silver wrote an article for Refinery29 about how "[When you're single, you're] nobody's number one. [You] don't have a natural, assumed partner for the basics, and [you] don't have someone to share joy with in the special moments. It's a really untethered feeling."

That pain, that longing, that hard truth without the soft pillow is fucking *real*. I'm all for choosing hope and joy, channeling relentless optimism and consciously reframing damn near everything to make the best of it, Emotional-Alchemy-style.

And still? *Sometimes life is just hard.*
Period.

Even when we *know* there's going to be a reason for the season, we *know* that pain is fleeting, we *know* that we can absolutely use our suffering as a vehicle for expansion, *it's also critically important to be honest* about our feelings and fears.[8]

If you feel or have ever felt the sting of not being anyone's number one, I see you, and I stand with you in hardship of that moment.

Earlier we talked about ritualizing sadness, and you now know what that looks like in a very practical, hands-on, and tangibly beautiful way, unique to you, specifically. Now that you have that knowledge, skillset, and permission to use it, let's drop into the more ethereal way of what it means to hold the vision and trust the process.

You already know what it feels like to see repeating numbers on the clock. Feathers on the ground. Dimes left on the sidewalk when you're out for a walk.

You already know that feeling of running into someone you were *just*

---

8 Which is exactly what we do in *To Call Myself Beloved: A Story of Hope, Healing, and Coming Home.*

thinking about. Seeing that thing pop up on your social feeds that you were *just* talking about to your friend. Having that conversation come up with someone randomly that you were *literally just talking about last week* with your family.

You already know the wonder that comes from the tarot, human design, or astrological reading that leaves you in tears because *it's exactly what you needed to hear* right now.

And I bet *you already know how lovely it is to have those synchronicities in your life.*

What if those little synchronicities aren't synchronicities at all? What if they're milestone markers or what I call "cosmic breadcrumbs" left out for you to follow along your path as you go?

What if each of them offers a little insight (and then a little more) about being hot or cold with respect to alignment with exactly where you're supposed to be at exactly the right time, even when it's hard, over and over and over again?

That theme of "not being chosen" was, as you know, prevalent as a limiting belief and decision for so much of my life, so when I chose to choose myself, or rather chose to acknowledge that *I'd already chosen* myself, it was a huge breakthrough in my own emotional, and frankly spiritual, sovereignty.

So, that day that I went out to the woods to effectively formalize the union I had with myself was kind of an emotional, and spiritual, power move.

And then the craziest thing happened.

The weekend my friend Nina and I went up to the cabin, another friend had invited me out for coffee. When I told her I was booked, she told me she first thought, "Oh right, she's busy that weekend because she's meeting THE guy," harkening back to a *vivid* dream she'd had previously of me and a big, burly, bearded guy with a man bun, together in buffalo plaid and denim jackets at a flower stand in a farmer's market.

I'll take it.

Anyway, she recounted this story to me, and I laughed. "Sure. Maybe this is the weekend—in the middle of the woods—when I'll meet the guy."

The day of the self-commitment ceremony, I was getting ready while Nina, talented photographer that she is, felt compelled to go offsite from our cabin to scout a better location for photos. Just before she left, and while I was changing into my dress—the first dress I'd worn in my post-chemo (read: much weight gain) and post-mastectomy (read: wildly disproportionate) body—I started to have some pretty big feelings.

Women's bodies are designed to evolve; mine had just evolved so quickly that I didn't have time to catch up. And changing into this little white cotton shift dress was kind of painful—realizing my body didn't look anything like it used to, it took me a moment to recenter myself.

Tempted to call it quits entirely, or to just do the ceremony in jeans and a flower crown, I listened as Nina gently reminded me that it's okay to grieve, and it's okay to still make this day special. She said, "Wear whatever you want and whatever you feel most comfortable in; imagine that the big, burly, bearded man of your dreams walks out of the woods after chopping wood, and he sees you. What do you want him to see you wearing? *How would you show up as yourself?*"

I wiped away my tears, laughed, and said, "Thank you for the reframe, and for bringing back the sacred nature of the self-commitment ceremony. Thank you for that compassionate call out, and for making me check in with what is really important. And also, thank you for holding that ridiculously vulnerable and honest space for me. And to answer your question? Sure, if Mr. Wonderful walks out of the woods while we're doing this ceremony here up north, in the middle of nowhere, then I definitely want him to see me in this dress."

Decision made.
Off she went to find a cool location; off I went to finish getting ready.

While I was dusting on some bronzer, curling my hair, and adjusting the flower crown on my head, Nina returned and joined me in the bathroom to tell me she'd found the *perfect* spot just minutes away.

So, we adjusted our plan to do the ceremony in the woods at the cabin, packed up the car, and headed back to the spot she found just moments before. And she was right; it was perfect. It was a huge, rocky, moss-covered cliff scape, beautifully wooded with birch and cedar.

From the top of the rock, I could see Otter Lake on one side and a smaller, more private-looking lake on the other. As we stood there, taking it in and planning out where we'd set up for the ceremony, we heard male voices.

We looked down to the bottom of the cliff's cape where—I kid you not—a big, burly, bearded man and his friend were literally *walking out of the woods*. I couldn't breathe. Nina couldn't breathe. We just stood there, speechless.

This booming but gentle voice said, "You guys okay up there?"
"Oh yeah, we're great, how are you?"
"Yeah, I'm doing great except for the fact that you're on my property. I own this."

Cue the instant and honest apologies from Nina and me.
"Uh, do you mean . . . we're *trespassing?*"

Bearded guy laughs. "Yeah. You are. But go ahead and use it. I really don't care. Just please don't get hurt. Please stay safe. It's a little bit slippery up there. And I just want you to be safe."

We manage to choke out a thank you (I get even nerdier than usual in the presence of good-looking men) and ask his name (Ben), then back into the woods he went, down a little hill.

I was dying of joy.

I was in complete disbelief that that experience had just happened. Completely gob smacked, I looked at Nina and just started laughing. *What. The actual. Fuck. Just happened.*

"Uh, did a hot bearded guy *really* just walk out of the woods?"
It was uncanny.

Nina went back to the car to get some of our props, and I stayed up at the top to set them up, when all of a sudden I heard music playing, loudly and distinctly, where there hadn't been music before. I stopped what I was doing to pause and listen for a minute, and all I heard was that classic Bobby McFerrin whistle, followed by the classic Bobby McFerrin singing, "Don't Worry, Be Happy."

And then it faded away.
I couldn't make up this shit if I tried.[9]

I stood there as a feeling of deep peace and calm flooded my entire body and being. Here I was, making a soulful declaration to *choose me*. I chose to be in loving partnership with myself. Exactly as I am, to death do us part.

And a fucking *bearded man* walks out of the woods, only to be followed by one verse of *the* song that came "out of nowhere" telling me not to worry.

....

9 Unless, of course, I have already written it into the screenplay of my life and now I'm just acting it out in real time. JUST saying . . .

Relief.

Sweet, divine relief.

After the ceremony, as Nina and I headed back to our cabin, we scoped out the little hill that Ben and Co had walked down; it was a driveway that led to the *midcentury modern cabin he was building on the water*. Like, this man was building *my* dream home, by himself, on the water. And the address was number 22, which for me, already holds spiritual significance as a marker of alignment.

Does that mean that Ben and I fell madly in love and lived happily ever after? No, because I checked the building permit and Ben was *definitely* building it for his wife.

The takeaway was that I had made a declaration of doing what felt good, what brought me joy, what was fun, what was pleasurable, and what I felt passionate about and really celebrating it all. And in doing so? I gave my subconscious the *conscious* proof that *what I want exists*. And that maybe, just maybe, I'm allowed to *have* what I want.

It was like God handed down one of those hotel room service trays with the big silver dome, and I opened it up to reveal that I'd been gifted with an almost identical replica—another actual physical manifestation—of *exactly what I want* the moment I chose to choose me.

It was a cosmic breadcrumb of a glimmer of hope telling me that what I want exists, *and* what I want exists *right now*. Even if it hasn't made its way to my life yet, here was the trailer of another part of the movie of my life that was coming soon.

Magic.

Hard truth, soft pillow?
This is bigger than you.

This. All of this.

We want to think we have so much control over circumstance, timing, and outcome, which creates a tremendous amount of pressure to perform. To do it all perfectly. To create and then adhere to a timeline that you alone control. And when it doesn't work out on time or in the way you planned? It feels like a crushing failure.

But this is bigger than you.
It's bigger than me.
It's bigger, and far more connected, than any of us can really understand.

Imagine a tangled ball of yarn that looks like a hundred different strands, all coming at you from different directions and in complete chaos. But when you mindfully slow down, find one end, and lovingly (if painstakingly) unwrap it from the entanglement that is the hot mess of a knot, it becomes almost glaringly obvious that *it's just one thread.*

I think our lives are like that.

We feel so alone, so isolated, like we are the *only ones* having those feelings of alone-ness and isolation, which then makes us feel more separate. Living in rounds of global lockdown for over a year really exacerbated those feelings. Not only did the pandemic force us to slow down and be in our own stillness, it removed so many of our false coping mechanisms we use to "deal with" those feelings of alone-ness and isolation.

In my one-on-one work with clients, I have this beautifully intimate front-row seat to their own experiences all over the world. And from those experiences? I can tell you that we are all having the *same emotional human experience.*

Yes, it manifests differently in our lived and physical experiences, but at the core, the emotional experience and process is. the. same.

We are *so* much more connected than we know. We need to wrap our heads around the fact that we are like seven billion little drops of water that are individual when seen on their own, but really, all together, they are an ocean. And each ocean is actually bazillions of tiny little individual drops of water.

We can feel alone in our overwhelming separateness, and we can also choose to appreciate that we are *never* alone in our overwhelming togetherness.

Nature is a phenomenal mirror for our own life experience: nothing, literally nothing, is there by accident. Every plant, critter, and creature has a specific role to play in supporting their unique ecosystem. What arrogance is required to think that humans aren't a part of that? That we somehow supersede every other living organism on the planet?

If you are here, you are here for a reason: a divinely held and supported reason.

Sometimes that reason makes perfect sense, and we dance.
We celebrate. We feel invincible in our joy.

Sometimes that reason makes no sense at all, and we doubt.
We question. We feel overwhelmed in our sorrow.

What if you zoomed out?

What if you allowed yourself to truly feel a part of something bigger, even (and particularly) in those seasons of fear and doubt, and allow yourself to look for, find, and be found by those little cosmic breadcrumbs telling you that you're still on the right path.

Think of your own life as a movie, one that you are simultaneously watching and living:
When you go through those really hard seasons, imagine a team of writers in an LA bungalow, coming up with the overall pilot and subplot of your life, working on the characters, character development, strategic foreshadowed elements, soundtrack (obvi), distractions, diversions, wins, losses, and pinnacle challenges that lead to your most triumphant moments.

Sometimes you may want to fire the team of writers and scream, "Get to the fucking point already!"

Sometimes they may make you laugh so hard you can't even believe how talented they are.

Sometimes they hand you a subplot that brings so much beauty and joy that you just marvel at the wonder of it all.

And sometimes, when you think they've been getting a litttttle too creative in that season seven slump and have lost their way, say to yourself, "This is just an off season. I can't wait to see what they have planned next; I can't wait for the comeback."

Because it is planned, planned even accounting for the missteps of free will.
It is all for a reason, and it is not random.

And if it's not random, then there is at least some semblance of structure and direction that you are divinely guided to follow, being supported all the while, gathering up the little cosmic breadcrumbs along the way.

What if you could gently explore the fact that ultimately, single, coupled, or somewhere in between, you are your own number one. I cannot say this enough:
The pain is so real of feeling alone in the experience of not feeling like someone else's number one, of not feeling chosen.

When you allow yourself to see the divine forest through the trees, your own path becomes clearer and more abundantly alive, and you are allowed to choose yourself over and over again, and to have that be enough for you.

It is enough for you to belong to yourself.

And when you belong to yourself, the truth and beauty of it is that you are never really alone.

CHAPTER TWENTY-TWO

LEAP

I am not afraid of heights, but I *am* afraid of falling.

I realized that fear several years ago when I happened to find an actual, old-timey swimming hole, in the middle of a provincial park, on a beautiful summer day.

It was idyllic; families were out playing and picnicking, and people of all ages, from four-year-old kids to sixty-four-year-old guys, were climbing up to the top of a fifteen-foot rock and leaping off into the calm black water below.

I was fine to climb up on the rocks, and I wanted *all* the joy I could see that would come from jumping off the edge into that calm water. But I was *terrified* of actually making that leap and *terrified* by the fear of the pain of falling into the unknown.

I stood there, overthinking this realization in my head, the one that told me I was too afraid to stay where I was and miss out on the possibility of what could be, *and* I was too afraid to leave the comfort of where I was (in the safety of how predictable and known it was) to leap.

It hit me that this little realization on the rocks wasn't just about deciding to literally leap or not to leap, it was the mirror of an *epic* decision I was wrestling with in my head: to *metaphorically* leap or not to leap into a terrifying next chapter of my life called "divorce."

It hit me that the decision I made right there on those rocks would be *the* decision I made in my real life, and I became paralyzed with fear.

I stood there on top of the rocks for what must have been *at least* two hours. Standing. Deliberating. Silently debating. Getting close to the edge and then pulling myself back to where I felt safe again.

Staying where I was meant to stay in the safety and comfort of what was known, even if what was known was lonely and unhappy. There was a part of me that really didn't want to disrupt that. Leaping off the edge meant listening to my gut and trading the safety and comfort (even if it was lonely and unhappy) for the wild exhilaration of the possibility and joy of *what could be*.

I knew the risk was high; I knew (in my heart) the reward would be great.

After two hours of being completely unable to make a decision, fearing that each one would be the wrong one, I knew suddenly in an instant, without any warning, that I was ready. I remember having a flash of courage and knowing, *knowing* what I needed to do.

And so, I leapt.
I free-fell all the way down, which was, in fact, unsettling and even scary until I found a safe haven in the water below.

And the water was divine.

The reward of being in the warm, sparkling water surrounding me was worth the stomach-turning fear of falling into it. I had unwaveringly made the right decision. And not long after that day, my decision to leap in my life was reflected from my decision to leap off the rocks.

In both cases, it was scary.
In both cases, it was really hard to be in a free fall.
And in both cases, the reward of inner peace made it worth the risk.

Your turn:

What is it that you need to do that you most do not want to do?
What is your fear telling you, and what is your fear masking?
Which part of you needs your permission to be?

Where in your life is it required for you to find the courage to *leap?*

Sometimes the leap looks like making a sweeping change, a dramatic gesture that radically alters the course of your life. And sometimes, actually more often, the leap looks like quiet, subtle shifts in your beliefs, thoughts, and eventually behaviors that allow you to trust yourself to do what's right.

Sometimes the biggest leap of all is to shift patience *into* presence *and allow it to be what it is.*

Let yourself off the hook of needing to control all the people, environments, and circumstances of your life. Give yourself permission to do what feels good in your heart, even if what feels good in your heart is by no means easy.

This is the leap.

This book started as an idea to offer solace and comfort to people who, like me, felt alone in a season of being single. And as it materialized, the more people I shared it with, the more it became strikingly obvious that being alone has almost nothing to do with being single and almost everything to do with how we feel about being alone with our Self.

There is so much unknown in our lives. So much mystery. So much bad advice on how you navigate the mystery of that unknown. The intention of this book evolved into exploring the beautiful truth that *alone and lonely are not the same thing,* nor are they mutually exclusive.

There can be profound pain in feeling lonely when you're right next to someone, and there can be profound peace in solitude when absolutely no one else is around.

Being not only comfortable but also *joyful* in your own company is a gift you alone can give to yourself, and in doing so, it is a gift you offer to each and every relationship you have moving forward, in your work, life, family, and love.

This is the leap.

If you are looking for the feeling of completion or wholeness from someone or something else, you have to, *have to* find a way of cultivating that completion on your own. That is a huge ask and a huge task for many, if not most of us. It goes against cultural programming, and frankly, it goes against even some of our biological instincts. I promise you, taking the time to *learn and know* yourself will set you up for a lifetime of inner peace and calmness.

Zeroing in on the reality that the relationship you have with yourself is *the* foundation upon which you build every other relationship will give you the permission to be so comfortable in who you are that when the timing is right for your next relationship, in any area of your life, you'll be able to *be in* the full expression of who you are *while* attracting a person who is comfortable with themselves too.

Terri Cole once told me I was a delicious piece of cake all on my own and that anyone else who came into my intimate life would simply be the icing.

You are the cake.
Anyone else is the icing.

Part of being alone is baking that cake. Meticulously choosing ingredients. Maybe trying out a few different recipes until you find the one that best reflects who you are.

This is the leap.

Hard truth, soft pillow: There is no *one* universal recipe and no *one* magic formula except knowing that the magic formula is that we are all figuring it out and that there is no real endpoint. Every one of us is in a process of self-creation. The human experience is about self-creation, self-awareness, and self-recognition in the pursuit of joyful connection to yourself.

You are allowed to be alone and desire company.
You are allowed to have company and desire solitude.
You are allowed to take time getting to know you.
You are allowed to set boundaries that protect you *while* being in a relationship with anyone else.
It's not either/or, it's both/and.

This is the leap.

Because you're reading these words right now, use them as cosmic breadcrumbs that are confirming that everything that has come before was the way that it was so that everything that comes next can be what it is.

You are literally in the perfect place at the perfect time of your life, even if it doesn't make sense yet.

What if there's no guidebook for a reason?
What if there is no right way?
What if there is no wrong way?
What if there's just *your* way?

What if every single experience you've had to date is exactly, *exactly* what you needed at the time to bring you here in this moment?
What if this moment is exactly what you need in order to move forward into the next moment after that?
What if it's all connected and is unfolding in perfect timing, even if that timing is making us stir-crazy or doubtful?

How freeing would it be to know that every decision you make *is* the right decision for you?

This is the leap.

This is what it means to be a human:
- It's to live in the both/and, not having to choose either/or.
- It's being both incredibly confused *and* incredibly tuned in.
- It's appreciating the simplicity *while* appreciating the complexity.
- It's feeling so concrete *while* feeling so ethereal.
- It's acquiring a lifetime of wisdom and being comfortable in knowing that that wisdom is yours for a reason.

Could you love yourself enough to simply revel in the *wow*?

Could you love yourself enough to inject a level of playfulness and joy where there used to be overthinking or anxiety?

Could you love yourself enough to truly make this experience your own and not only share but also celebrate the experience that others around you are having in a similar but different way?

Could you love yourself enough to detach from outcome or from judging that things are good or bad and accepting that they just are?

This is the leap.

My first book was the instruction manual of HOW TO love and accept yourself, and my intention for *this* book is to pick up where *To Call Myself Beloved* left off: to answer the brutally honest question of *"Now what?"*

Now that I love myself, what do I do, especially if I didn't get the cookie I was hoping for when I learned TO love myself? And what does that look like in each of those areas of my existence, from work to life to love?

If the relationship you have with yourself is the most important one and is the foundation upon which all other relationships are built, now you know the secret of what it means to simultaneously be alone and belong to yourself, no matter where you are or who you are with, or who you are without.

Being able to embody the sovereignty of what it means to be alone and reclaim it as your own is paramount to *strengthening* the relationship you have with yourself. It then ripples, without question, into all other areas from work and money to life and love.

Which is what it means to belong to yourself.

Because when you belong to yourself, and especially when you can see your Self as a part of something much, much bigger than yourself, the truth and beauty of it is that you are never really alone.

TL; DR:

When you belong to yourself, the truth and beauty of it is that you are never really alone.

Have patience with everything that remains unsolved in your heart. Try to love the questions themselves . . . Do not now look for the answers. They cannot be given to you because you could not live them. It is a question of experiencing everything. At present you need to live the question. Perhaps you will gradually, without even noticing it, find yourself experiencing the answer, some distant day.

–Rainer Maria Wilke

RESOURCES AND WORKS CITED
(IN THE ORDER THEY APPEAR IN THE BOOK)

Maya Angelou, interview by Bill Moyers, *Bill Moyers Journal*, November 21, 1973. https://billmoyers.com/content/conversation-maya-angelou/

Walker, Pete. *Complex PTSD: From Surviving to Thriving*. Azure Coyote, 2013. http://pete-walker.com/

Tillich, Paul. *The Eternal Now*. Peter Smith Pub Inc., 1963.

Lexico.com

Wolfe, Thomas. *God's Lonely Man*. https://www.goodreads.com/work/quotes/63366416-god-s-lonely-man

Mitchell, Mike, dir. *Trolls*. Dreamworks, 2016. https://www.dreamworks.com/trolls

Chapman, Gary. *The 5 Love Languages*. Northfield Pub., 2015.

Traister, Rebecca. *All the Single Ladies: Unmarried Women and the Rise of an Independent Nation*. Simon & Schuster, 2016.

Abrell, Karin Anderson, PhD. *Single is the New Black: Don't Wear White 'til it's Right*. Clifton Hills, 2021.

Wilson, Lana, dir. *Miss Americana*. Netflix, January 31, 2020.

Tolstoy, Leo. *Family Happiness and Other Stories*. Dover, 2005. (reprint)

Mark Twain quote: https://www.goodreads.com/quotes/83918-the-worst-loneliness-is-to-not-be-comfortable-with-yourself

Piazza, Jo. *How to Be Married: What I Learned from Real Women on Five Continents About Building a Happy Marriage*. Harmony, 2017.

Elsie de Wolf quote: https://www.goodreads.com/quotes/51441-i-am-going-to-make-everything-around-me-beautiful--

Cole, Terri. *Boundary Boss: The Essential Guide to Talk True, Be Seen, and (Finally) Live Free*. Sounds True, 2021.

Silver, Shani. "What Happens When You're No One's Number One?" Refinery29, January 16, 2019. https://www.refinery29.com/en-us/2019/01/221284/being-single-no-ones-number-one

Wilke, Rainer Maria. *Letters to a Young Poet*. W.W. Norton and Company, 1954.

WITH GRATITUDE

Fun fact: Nothing pulls you out of the melancholy of feeling alone like taking a hard look at all the people who've made it possible for you to be where you are:

Thank you for letting me into your life via your bookshelf and for trusting me enough to share this little corner of the universe with you; I truly hope you found yourself in these pages and took what you needed in this moment to move forward.

Thank you to Sabrina and the YGTM team for taking what—for quite some time—was just an idea circling around my head and turning it into *this*: a 60,000-word love letter to anyone anywhere who's ever felt that slow burning sting of being alone and wondered what the hell to do about it.

Thank you to the real-life versions of the pseudonyms in these pages for the reasons, seasons, and lessons you offered, and particularly to the beautiful friendships who have held a lot of space for me to process a lot of feelings out loud and in VM, and who have been deliciously present in moments of genuine connection.

Thank you to my sweet Mia, Grey, and Clara for holding onto the ginger-bread-making, treehouse-building, into-the-lake-throwing, thing-fixing, BBQ-grilling, lame-joke-telling, outdoor-movies-on-a-screen-watching, piggybacking, family-adoring, *ultra-shamooshy-dog-owning* vision we've been dreaming of for oh so long; whoever he is, and whenever he gets here, he's going to be so lucky to have *you*.

Thank you to my amazing family for being so supportive of me professionally and personally; thank you especially to my aunts Corrie and Hilda for your respective and unique abilities to always pick up the phone when I call and for knowing exactly when to call me, sharing so much compassionate, caring wisdom each time.

ABOUT THE AUTHOR

Leisse Wilcox is a Conscious Relationship Coach and Mentor with expertise in finding truth and beauty in the relationships we have with ourselves and others.

As a Master Success Coach and best-selling author of *To Call Myself Beloved: A Story of Hope, Healing, and Coming Home*, she is changing the global conversation on emotional health and self-love. She has been interviewed in media including *Entrepreneur*, Refinery29, CNN, Elephant Journal, the *Toronto Star*, and Thrive Global.

A passionate (and TEDx) speaker, dynamic thought leader, author, NLP practitioner, top podcast host, cancer survivor, solo parent of three, and taco enthusiast, Leisse knows intimately that every relationship we have, in business, life, and love, is built on the foundation of the relationship we have with ourselves.

Head to LeisseWilcox.com to connect with her one on one.

@leissewilcox
LeisseWilcox.com
How to Be a Human: The Podcast with Leisse Wilcox
Leisse Wilcox

YGTMedia Co. is a blended boutique publishing house for mission-driven humans. We help seasoned and emerging authors "birth their brain babies" through a supportive and collaborative approach. Specializing in narrative nonfiction and adult and children's empowerment books, we believe that words can change the world, and we intend to do so one book at a time.

ygtmedia.co/publishing

@ygtmedia.co

@ygtmedia.co

CPSIA information can be obtained
at www.ICGtesting.com
Printed in the USA
LVHW081023120322
713305LV00026B/525